THE SPEED OF DARK

THE SPEED OF DARK

A Memoir

By

JORAM PIATIGORSKY

Adelaide Books
New York / Lisbon
2018

The Speed of Dark
a memoir
by Joram Piatigorsky

Copyright © 2018 By Joram Piatigorsky

Cover design & Interior formatting © 2018 Adelaide Books
Cover images and all images throughout the book are
from the Author's Personal Archive

Published by Adelaide Books, New York / Lisbon
adelaidebooks.org

Editor-in-Chief
Stevan V. Nikolic

For any information, please e-mail Adelaide Books
at info@adelaidebooks.org
or write to:
Adelaide Books
244 Fifth Ave. Suite D27
New York, NY, 10001

ISBN13:   978-1-949180-53-4
ISBN10: 1-949180-53-0

Printed in the United States of America

To the memory of my parents,
who gave me my foundation,
and to my cherished family – Lona, Auran and Anton.

"The experience that lasted an instant plays out for a lifetime inside us." - *Pico Iyer*

Contents

Preface

One of the most important and life-saving events of my existence occurred before I was born, when my parents and two-year-old sister, Jephta, boarded the *Isle de France* on September 1, 1939, in Le Havre, destined for America. Due to the threat of war, my parents endured two anxious – frightening – days moored in the harbor while the ship's captain considered whether or not to risk the dangerous ocean journey. What if the ship was torpedoed? On September 3, the day France and England declared war on Nazi Germany, he took the gamble.

The stamp in Papa's Nansen Passport – a stateless certificate of identity given to refugees by the League of Nations – confirms that my parents arrived in New York on September 9. Safe!

Five months later, on February 4, 1940, genetically half French and half Russian, I was born in upstate New York, becoming the first American citizen in my European family. My parents became naturalized American citizens a few years later. Ironically, the forced immigration from war-torn Europe turned out to be an unintended gift that initiated my secure American future.

I switched from speaking French at home to speaking English when I started school and was raised under the influence of my parents' European culture, not unlike many other Jewish immigrants of the time. But that's where the similarity ended. Mama, Jacqueline Rebecca Louise de Rothschild, was the daughter of Baron Édouard de Rothschild of the French banking dynasty, and Papa, Gregor Piatigorsky, was a world-renowned Russian cellist. Thus, I had the financial security of a Rothschild heir, with exposure to their extra-ordinary art collections and lavish lifestyle, and the name recognition of Papa's celebrity status as a cellist. From birth, the extraordinary was ordinary in my family. Unlike other memoirs about rising from adversity to achieve success, mine is about clearing a high bar set by my unique family, challenging me to find my own distinct voice.

I broke the chain of my European lineage of art, music and banking by pursuing a career in science in America. This is my story of research in vision and genetics, influenced by my background of artists.

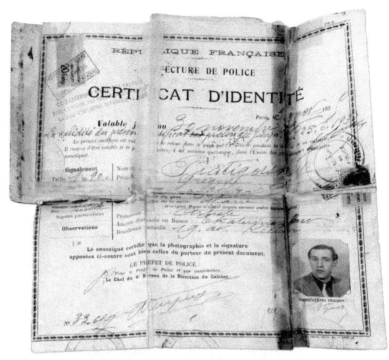

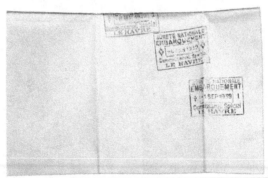

The Nansen Certificate of Papa showing the dates he boarded the ship in Le Havre (September 1, 1939) and arrived in New York (September 9, 1939) escaping the war in Europe.

The Great PIATIGORSKY

NOW PLAYING HIS GALA 10TH ANNIVERSARY AMERICAN TOUR

13 APPEARANCES IN 6 SEASONS WITH THE BOSTON SYMPHONY

"To say that Piatigorsky was at his best is merely to say that nothing in the way of 'cello playing could possibly have been better."

Warren Storey-Smith,
Boston Post: January 28, 1939

18 APPEARANCES IN 8 SEASONS WITH THE CHICAGO SYMPHONY

"Indeed an enormous favorite here. . . . It took 8 leisurely recalls to silence an undiminished stream of applause."

Eugene Stinson, Chicago Daily News: January 20, 1939

"Spectacular endowments. . . . Here his instrument sang as artlessly as a child, there it took on the great resonance necessary to convey the music's drive and passion. Between these extremes were countless sun-touched colorings of a subtle and indescribable beauty."

Edward Barry, Chicago Tribune: January 20, 1939

3rd SEASON WITH THE DETROIT SYMPHONY

"He evokes the angels . . . gave such an exhibition of virtuosity and emotional sweep that he commanded a breathless attention which broke into insistent applause at the end of each movement, and at the close became a genuine ovation."

Ralph Holmes, Detroit Evening Times: February 3, 1939

Available Next Season

JANUARY 22 TO APRIL 10, 1940

CONCERT MANAGEMENT, ARTHUR JUDSON, INC.

Division of Columbia Concerts Corporation of Columbia Broadcasting System

Victor Records

News clipping announcing Papa's American tour in 1940
after escaping the war in Europe, 1940.

In the Audience

Papa held his Stradivarius cello high with his arm extended, his hand gripping its neck as he bounded onto the stage to eager audiences. When he played, he enveloped the cello with his bear-like body and tilted his head towards the scroll, becoming one with his precious instrument. The music flowed as if it came from his soul. That was my Papa that the audience knew and loved.

I remember accompanying him with Mama in 1967 in my final year as a graduate student at Caltech to the Pablo Casals Music Festival in Puerto Rico. One afternoon at the beach, knee-deep in the tepid seawater, I heard Papa and the Indian-born conductor, Zubin Mehta, talk of their inspiration to replace their scheduled concert of the Dvorak cello concerto the next day with the Don Quixote cello concerto by Richard Strauss.

"But it's not on the agenda for the festival, Grisha," Mehta said, calling Papa by the nickname used by his family and close friends. "We don't even have the music. When will we practice?"

Mehta called his father, also a conductor in California, and asked him to send the music express mail; an impromptu rehearsal took place hours before the concert.

I sat amongst the audience next to Mama, tapped my fingers self-consciously upon my knee and watched the empty seats become occupied. I felt anxious, although I didn't know why, since Papa's performances were always flawless to my ears. When the audience had filled all the seats, extra chairs were placed on the stage. TV cameras were located strategically for local broadcasting. The spontaneous concert was a rare treat – one for the books – that was going to be shared throughout the island.

Papa marched on the stage, cello held high as usual, looking imperious. Did he hold the cello above his head to protect it from being knocked, or was it humility, symbolic in that he was a servant of music, not its master, and that the sacred cello chose him – not the other way around?

Papa claimed the single, featured chair – a throne upon a small platform on the stage in front of the orchestra. Mehta stiffened, prepared to conduct. Applause, and then a great hush, heavy as the humidity.

Papa projected confidence, and I felt pride to be his son.

In the seconds before the music started I imagined him thinking, "What a crazy idea to play the Don Quixote concerto, unprepared, on the spur of the moment."

Not crazy, I thought. Runaway enthusiasm often poured from him, like his dreams to explore jungles, to search for burial grounds of elephants, or to plummet the depths of the oceans to witness its mysteries. He had often told me how lucky I was to learn so much at college, which he had never attended (he hadn't even gone to high school), and how I would have great adventures in my life. It was almost as if he envied me! Did he expect me to live his dreams?

Was I destined for the audience and not the stage?

Papa scanned the audience, and I imagined he caught sight of me, a speck in the sea of faces. Suddenly I felt anxious again, as if I too was on stage, with a great responsibility on my shoulders.

Mehta lowered the baton and the orchestra commenced. Papa entered with a bold stroke of his bow. He closed his eyes, swayed, and transformed his cello into Don Quixote, bantered with Sancho Panza, the violist, charged the windmill, and fantasized his love for Dulcinea. I too closed my eyes and retreated within myself. Simultaneously, I became Papa, the famous cellist; Don Quixote, an idealist with illusions larger than life; and myself, a student scientist, Papa's son, a spectator in the audience, feeling both big and small, but with an artist's heart that only I could sense.

At a momentary lull for Don Quixote, Papa's face grew taut. He tightened the bow hairs, wiped his forehead, and shifted his feet and cello. My anxiety returned. I remembered the times I woke at night, dreaming that I was on stage and had forgotten the notes.

Captured by my imagination, I heard Papa say, "I've played this piece a thousand times, even discussed it with Strauss (this was true); now I can't remember all the notes. It would be terrible if I messed up, especially before my son. No, it would be worse than that: it would be a tragedy."

Really? Would it be a tragedy for him, or a tragedy for me?

"I'm not good enough," Papa muttered in my mind.

Was I listening to Papa's voice, or my own?

I relaxed again when the music continued. Did I really think Papa would flub his performance? Even if he had a transient lapse of memory on stage, the world was still in his pocket. He would improvise and few, if any, would realize his gaffe. He was a survivor, and a master musician.

The final passages carried Don Quixote to a beautiful, quiet death. The battle was over, at least for Don Quixote and Papa. No more windmills to combat, no more demons to avoid.

Papa sat still. Mehta sighed. The audience remained silent for a moment, the highest form of praise, and then applause, whistles and a standing ovation.

"Bravo!" echoed throughout the theater. I applauded, suspended on a cloud. But shouting bravo was too conspicuous for me, too self-serving, like announcing, "I'm here too." Cheering publicly felt embarrassing, improper, like cheering for myself. But how could I feel that way, when I also felt invisible?

Papa wiped his brow, stood and bowed. He hugged Mehta. Mehta hugged him back, an exclusive union no one else could join – not a friend, not Mama, not me.

A man in front of me said, "Magic." His wife nodded in agreement.

Magic? No, I thought. It was food for the hungry.

I rushed backstage with Mama to greet Papa, who was soaked in perspiration as he came off the stage, the applause from the audience subsiding.

"Zubin's a genius," Papa said, to no one in particular.

"You played phenomenally," I said. "Fantastic. Incredible."

Artists speak in superlatives. I wanted to be understood. I meant it, and more. The more part was harder to get across.

"Thank you," he replied. "I hope you liked it."

He drifted towards the growing crowd to greet friends and fans. Mama and I waited in the corner of the dressing room as admirers paid their respects, one by one.

I heard Papa saying, "M-i-l-i-c-h-k-a, kidkins, what a surprise! I had no idea that you were here," in his Russian accent.

Occasionally someone congratulated me in the corner.

"Thank you," I responded, feeling uncomfortable to be praised undeservedly for accomplishments of others, even Papa's.

"You must be proud of your father," they said.

"Yes," I answered, because that was true.

I wondered what Papa might be thinking as he gesticulated with enthusiasm, spoke a lot of Russian, laughed at jokes, hugged old friends and made new ones. Did he really feel like the king holding court? Who were the jesters, who the noblemen? And if he saw himself a king, why did he complain so often about the profession, or anguish about the critics – his constant demons?

"I love music," he had said, "but not the career, not the life of a musician."

As I saw him conquer crowds and individuals with skill and charm, he spoke again in my mind: "Hotels, concerts, constant effort my whole life, since I was eight, no, six, who knows? And the critics, who can't play a note themselves, but dare to judge me."

There you have it: he was both king and serf.

Mama and I waited for the last few stragglers to leave. Mama signaled Papa when she had enough. She was always impatient, even more than me.

Yes, he signaled back, I know. But then he spoke some more. We waited.

My mind replayed his coming off the stage, as if it were a video.

Papa said: "Zubin's a genius."

I answered: "You played phenomenally. Fantastic. Incredible."

Papa replied: "Thank you. I hope you liked it."

Then he touched my cheek before he turned to greet the crowd.

Mama and Papa in September, 1937.

Grigor Piatigorsky jouant à la fenêtre du château
de Ferrières pour sa fille qui était en bas —

Papa playing the cello in the window of Château de Ferriere serenading
Jephta who was a few months old (below, not seen), circa 1938.

Château de Ferrière estate grounds, circa 1940s.

I'm sitting next to Joli Garçon painting by Chaim Soutine, circa 1958.

Joli Garçon

Traditionally, Papa played chamber music at home each New Year's Eve, a ritual – more a superstition – to avoid bad luck in the coming year. The great Russian-born violinist Jascha Heifetz was always included. The pianist Leonard Pennario was usually there, the violist William Primrose a few times, and always a small contingent of fine musicians who lived in the area. I remember Polish-American pianist Arthur Rubinstein came a few times in the early days. These gatherings at our home, and occasionally at Heifetz's, were cast as an informal group of friends playing chamber music, but the evening was hardly informal or ordinary. I felt the tension of a formal concert: elegant dress and no speaking or even whispering during the music. Mama would rush to the next room to pick up the receiver if the phone rang so as not to disturb the musicians.

The atmosphere overflowed with reverence for the musical perfection! The guests knew that they were privileged to be a part of such a distinguished gathering of musicians performing in the privacy of the artist's home. Of course, being the loyal, trusted friends of these great musicians was unique in itself.

For me those musical evenings weren't privileged or special. I didn't need an invitation. I remained after the guests went home, and I slept in my bed upstairs. My home was a concert hall at those times, where the ticket was free, where Mama and I were once again in the audience, and Papa was the cellist. My sister Jephta floated among the guests. At times I felt at home at these occasions, at other times more a stranger, restrained, unsure of what to say to the guests.

"Fantastic? Incredible?" What could I say?

I wasn't a musician and felt false in making any comments. My genuine love of the music, which was in fact both fantastic and incredible, was accompanied by a certain shame for not being a musician or playing an instrument. I felt as if I carried a flag that said, "I'm Not Important." I never considered that Papa's long-time friends and admirers weren't musicians and didn't play an instrument, or that little boys were not expected to be their parents.

If the music had made me feel sad or happy, I said, "It was beautiful." No more. If I had been bored, which was the case at times, I remained silent. When my mind drifted, as it often did and still does at concerts, I didn't tell anyone about my private thoughts. I was just a kid, after all.

Occasionally Papa and Heifetz, the dominant musicians in the group and center of attraction, would mutter comments or signal one another between notes that made them smile, or sometimes laugh, but I never understood the joke. I wasn't in the network. Also, they spoke mainly Russian, their native language, but foreign to me, a life apart from mine. Thus, home was partly a distant land famous for music I didn't play. Yet it was my home and natural in a way. I fit and didn't fit; it was wonderful, but not quite real;

it was extraordinary, but ordinary too, at least in my young mind.

Although quiet among the guests in the audience listening to the music, I had a pressing need to be understood. I felt that I had something important to express, but what exactly? I felt like kindling beneath logs for future flames in the fireplace with the flue still closed – an imprisoned artist with yet-to-be discovered potential.

Papa almost never spoke of music or about musicians at home. Music was always on a lofty plane for him. He didn't go to operas because he didn't like the acting interfering with the music. (I love opera.) He felt assaulted by background music.

"Having someone shove noise in your ears is no different than someone stuffing celery in your mouth when you're in a restaurant," he said.

Yet, despite his integrity for music as high art, he also saw the simple, non-scholarly human side. When someone hesitated to admit whether they liked a piece of music to avoid revealing ignorance, Papa would ask, "Would you ask a geologist if a mountain was beautiful?"

In Europe, well before the war, Papa bought Paul Klee paintings before Klee was famous, for trivial sums and gave them away as presents to his acquaintances, friends and colleagues. Papa loved all fine art. He was equally enthusiastic about an oil painting by Renoir of his wife and an ink drawing of a grotesque figure by José Luis Cuevas, a rebel Mexican artist who portrayed debased humanity, and he bought both before either was valuable. I never heard Papa mention value or consider art as investment or entertainment.

"Buy only what you love," he said. I understood that he also meant do only what you love, as he exemplified in music and his love of art. He acquired impressionist and expressionist paintings, African art, some ceramics and other creations that caught his fancy.

When I was seven years old Papa removed a rolled-up canvas, *The Man with a Felt Hat* by Chaim Soutine, from his suitcase, which he bought in Paris on tour in 1947. It was the first of four Soutine paintings that he would buy in his lifetime.

"Do you like *Joli Garçon?*" he asked. Papa made bonds by coining nicknames. *Joli Garçon* was thin, with orange hair and poorly aligned eyes, and a neatly knotted tie squeezing his scrawny neck. *Joli Garçon* – pretty boy – the subject in the painting, was Frank Burty Haviland in reality.

"Yes," I said cautiously. I liked it, but it was too much to comprehend and too scary to say more at my tender age. Yet, I felt Papa loved the painting, as if *Joli Garçon* was his new adopted child, perhaps an older brother for me, and he was showing me how important art was in his life.

Papa colored my view of art as personal and over time it infiltrated everything I did – science, collecting, writing. Like art, science required originality and experimentation, and was a form of self-expression, as personal as factual. Whatever I did, I made personal by seeing it as such. I respected knowledge, but I didn't seek a geologist to tell me whether the mountain was beautiful or ask a scholar to guide my taste in music or art. Papa taught me to trust my instincts – my whims and intuitions. If I felt I had something important to express, I took it seriously.

But my view of art wasn't limited to Papa's music or astute eye and love of art. Mama's connection with art shimmered like golden aspen leaves in the fall breeze and couldn't have been more different than Papa's.

Jascha Heifetz, Papa's close friend and a regular for chamber music at our home to celebrate the New Year as I grew up.

Mama holding me, Papa holding Jephta and grandparents (Grandpapa and Babushka) in Elizabethtown, 1940.

My parents (2nd and 3rd standing from left) at about the time they married (circa 1935) in Paris. To the right of Mama on the photo is her brother Guy and sister Bethsabée. Guy's wife (Alix) is sitting and her sister (Minka) is standing to the left of Papa.

Mama's parents, Babushka and Grandpapa, in Paris, circa 1955.

Palaces and Pogroms

"These penguins look so much at ease when they hop in and out of the frigid water," I said to my son, Anton, as we toured Antarctica in December 2000.

"Everywhere is home to someone," he answered.

There were penguins everywhere: Adelie penguins, Gentoo penguins, Chinstrap penguins. They were swift and graceful, leaping out of the water like airborne ballerinas. Multitudes of penguins stretched out in vast fields of rocks and ice and snow along the shore – a grandiose landscape of squawking penguins in the frozen paradise of Antarctica. Each penguin family, many with one or two newly hatched chicks, inhabited a circular nest of small rocks soiled with white excrement. The penguins waddled here and there, stealing rocks from their neighbors and adding them to their own nests, replacing those taken by another penguin. By trading rocks no penguin had a larger nest than any other.

As I watched this inane behavior – trading stolen rocks with no material gain – I thought about Mama, the daughter of Baron Édouard de Rothschild of the French banking family. Her background would make as little sense to penguins as their home in Antarctica made to me.

The Rothschilds acquired, they didn't trade, as the penguins do. My great-great grandfather, James (1792-1868), and my great grandfather, Alphonse (1827-1905) purchased the finest art. *(1-3)* Owning exquisite art for the Rothschilds was a badge of honor and privilege – an identity of excellence known as *le goût Rothschild* (the Rothschild taste). The art treasures turned their homes into private museums and were incorporated into their lifestyle, as an heirloom drawing by a beloved deceased grandparent might occupy a family den.

Summer visits to my grandparents in Paris after the war reinforced my French background. Those trips were multicolored: sparkling red for me, resentful blue for Mama and, I speculate, overcast gray for Papa. I loved the trans-Atlantic boat trips where I ran freely on the decks of ocean liners, saw movies and played ping-pong with Jephta. I relished the luxury of my grandparents' Parisian home, despite its formality and extensive staff, so different from our lifestyle in America. Their house was on Avenue Foch, a half block from the *Arc de Triomphe*.

As I wandered through my grandparents' home, Mama showed me all the art, stressing her favorites as she reverted to her childhood days. The place was virtually bursting with magnificent art on the walls, in cabinets and on antique tables. Imagine the scene: 16th century French Saint-Porchaire and Bernard Palissy pottery; 17th century French and Dutch paintings; 18th century *Sèvres* porcelain; Italian Renaissance jewelry; and historic French furniture. I loved riding the two private elevators in the halls – one elegant, the other utilitarian for servants – that connected the three floors. My bed stood out as the softest, most comfortable bed in the world. I forced myself to stay awake as long as possible between the silky sheets at night in order to enjoy the comforts longer. The warm chocolate croissants for breakfast, the tiny shrimps in their shells imported from *Maison Prunier* for lunch, and the gourmet dinners, although they dragged on for longer than a small boy would like, were delicacies that remained in my mind long after they had been digested.

Today I remember the formal dinners as relics from the elegant salons of Proust's era, attended by Rothschild relatives I never met. The place settings on the pristine tablecloths had Rothschild patterns on the Sevres plates. The blue and yellow colors of the designs, often birds, were the Rothschild colors worn by the jockeys when they raced the family's thoroughbred horses, a Rothschild tradition since the mid-19th century. Each place setting had a small dish of butter with the date stamped on the surface. Two Fragonard fantasy portraits – an Actor and an Actress – faced me as I had dinner in the dining room, and two Goya paintings – an aristocratic boy and an elegant girl looking like a princess – faced the Fragonard paintings on the opposite wall. I had no idea how rare and special these artworks were. All I understood was that they were part of my family, and it seemed natural to have dinners in their presence, as Mama did growing up. Footmen in white gloves served us on silver trays. I remember feeling clumsy when the food was present-ed to me on my left, which forced me to use my right hand to transfer the tasty morsels to my plate, an awkward motion, being left-handed. Another footman came around the table with a carafe filled with Château Lafite wine, whispering the vintage as he filled the crystal glass. My grandmother – we called her Babushka – rang a hand bell to let the servants waiting in the pantry know that we were ready for the next course.

While the servants in their formal attire seemed detached to me, they were Mama's confidants when she was a child. Having been tutored at home, she lacked playmates or friends. Also, instead of loving attention from her parents, she had a stern English nanny she detested. Mama felt closest to the servant Renée, who still worked for my grandparents when I first visited Paris. She was a gentle lady, who was genuinely happy to see Mama again and to meet Jephta and me. Years later, Mama drew a portrait of her, reproducing her face with precision and love.

After dinners we retreated to *le fumoir*, a cozy room adjacent to the dining room. We sank into plush sofas and chairs surrounded by art masterpieces. Several coffee tables – small antique treasures – were easily in reach for a candy, cookie, coffee or brandy.

The art, confiscated by the Nazis during the war for Hitler's unrealized *Führermuseum* in his Austrian hometown of Linz, took center stage in the house. I was given stern warnings to not throw things around that might damage any of the art! Miraculously, the stolen art was recovered after the war. Individual pieces from the collections have been donated to museums over time, but their Rothschild provenance remains. I remember feeling a personal connection with Johannes Vermeer's "The Astronomer" bought by my great-grandfather Alphonse de Rothschild in the later 19th century, when it flashed on the screen in the documentary movie *The Rape of Europa*, as a prized possession of Hitler's confiscated art. I saw this painting as a boy in my grandparents' home, and then again in the Louvre after it was given as payment for inheritance taxes in 1983. Having seen this picture in the family as a boy linked Vermeer's masterpiece with me at some level in my mind.

Nathan Mayer Rothschild, patriarch of the English branch of the Rothschild bank and son of my great-great-great grandfather, Mayer Amschel Rothschild, the founder of the Rothschild dynasty, claimed interest only in business, yet he boasted of his portrait collection to business associates. What more convincing voice than owning the most sought-after art could the Rothschilds have used for announcing their presence in the top echelons of society after they escaped the Frankfurt ghetto in the 18th century?

I saw relatively little of my grandfather – Grandpapa – on my summer trips to Paris. I made token appearances in his room to say a quick hello and goodbye. Grandpapa was sixteen years older than Babushka and in poor health; he never had meals with us. He had tuberculosis when he was younger, and I don't know if he ever was completely cured. Once, when one of his thoroughbred horses raced in Paris, I remember Grandpapa watching the event sitting in a wheelchair on top of his strategically parked car by the side of the racetrack. He was not strong enough to fight the crowds. We were all disappointed when "Violoncelle," the Rothschild horse named in honor of Papa, didn't win. Many years later, my uncle Guy named one of his racehorses "Lona" after my wife. Unfortunately, the horse never won a race and was put out to pasture.

I could never match the social ease of my cousin David, Guy's son, two years my junior. I tended to clam up in the

French society of my age group. Although I spoke French as a child, I couldn't keep up with the rapid exchanges, and the mannerisms and wit were too sophisticated for me. David, of course, was at home in this culture. I felt an outsider, belonging and yet not belonging, as if looking through a window and tapping on the glass.

I felt as American in France, as I felt French in America.

A highlight for me during our visits was staying in my grandparents' magnificent *Château de Ferrières* near Paris, built between 1855 and 1859 for Baron James de Rothschild, my great-great grandfather. Napoleon III attended its gala inauguration in 1862. The Germans seized it in the Franco-Prussian War of 1870-1871, and then the Nazis occupied it in the Second World War. The estate was like a small country village with a lake and cottages where, I believe, some of the domestic help lived. I loved bicycling throughout the wooded trails and exploring. The huge château had more rooms than I could keep track of. I remember discovering a secret passageway behind a hidden door in the hallway. The details have blurred with time, but the memories remain vivid: the splendor, the servants scurrying here and there, the polished glamour. This is where Mama was raised in lonely luxury and emotional poverty, and where Papa could never have imagined that he would ever set foot. These were my French grandparents, living an opulent, surreal existence in my American eyes.

Witnessing this slice of my heritage emphasized the extraordinary as everyday life, not unlike having Papa and Heifetz playing chamber music at home on New Year's Eve.

Yet, Rothschild riches and splendor had little to do with my ordinary life in America. My first few years were in

Elizabethtown, a small New York hamlet in the Adirondacks. Papa had bid on a rustic property – an Adirondack camp called Windy Cliff – in Elizabethtown during an earlier concert tour, probably anticipating the need for an escape from Europe in case of war. His bid was successful, and Papa, Mama and Jephta, went to Elizabethtown when they arrived as immigrants in America in 1939. I was born a few months later and became the first American citizen in my family. My parents became naturalized citizens there in 1942.

Windy Cliff – a Camelot to us – was nestled atop a scenic hill with a postcard view of the mountains, a stark contrast with my grandparents' existence in Paris. Mama felt "born again" in Elizabethtown, and beamed when she exclaimed, "I'm a Piatigorsky!" She had never even seen the kitchen in her childhood, but in Elizabethtown she cooked, shot porcupines that nibbled at the wood foundations of our house with her 22 gauge rifle, ice-skated on ponds (even a few hours before I was born!), played postal chess, taught herself the bassoon well enough to play in an amateur orchestra (she had played the piano in her youth as a student of the famous Alfred Corot), and whizzed along in a three-wheeler motorcycle, with Jephta and me in the side cart urging her, "Faster! Faster!" Despite Papa's fears, Mama even learned to pilot an airplane, but quit just before receiving her license after her teacher crashed in the Piper Cub she had flown, losing his life.

Elizabethtown was as unpretentious and informal as Paris was structured and formal. In the summers, Jephta and I picked sun-drenched wild blackberries in the meadows, eating a handful for each we put in the basket to take home for dinner. I learned to swim in the spring-fed, crystal-clear Bouquet River, often in the company of pigs that had wandered from the neighboring Otis farm. Jephta and I gobbled raw corn we stole from that farm, but never became sick. In the winter, I sank to my chest in the powder snow when I ventured out a few steps beyond our house. The frigid air was often well below zero, and we roasted marshmallows on a stick in the embers of a fireplace while sipping hot chocolate in the afternoons.

Elizabethtown was the foundation of my life, where I learned to love nature, and where Mama's liberation seeped into me.

Mama did not look forward to the family summer visits to France, which were filled with social engagements Babushka had prearranged and lengthy formal meals. However, she did have happy moments in Paris. I remember the day when she, Jephta and I slipped away for a few hours to explore Montmartre. We wandered along the alleyways full of charm and small shops, watched the artists paint in the streets, and ate bread and chocolate at a café. How Mama loved that afternoon. For her it was a "Roman Holiday," like the secret day-excursion for Audrey Hepburn in the movie by that name. But there were few such days for her in Paris.

From my perspective, Babushka was a gold mine! Each time I visited her, she took me, driven by her chauffeur, to Hermes (or occasionally another store) to buy whatever I wanted. What more could a growing boy want? I still have the gold wristwatch I chose, which reminds me of her every time I wear it.

Papa's childhood – rather a precocious adulthood – warrants a brief description for comparison with Mama's in palatial riches and security, for my identity resides between these two opposites.

Papa was born in Ekaterinoslav (now Dnepropetrovsk), Ukraine in 1904 (a recent discovery by Hamid Shams and Murray Grigor of Papa's birth certificate in Moscow revises the previously reported 1903 birthdate) into a life of hardships.*(4)*

"Blood ran in the streets," Papa said about the pogroms he endured as a boy. "I filled my pockets with rocks to protect myself from brutes that appeared at random and slaughtered Jews – men, women and children."

How could I, raised and sheltered in America, understand such terror? Impossible. No description of a pogrom could substitute for experiencing the real event.

Papa had two brothers (Leonid and Alexander; a third, Anatole, was born later) and two sisters (Pauline and Nadja), and music was a staple in his home. After the family moved to Moscow, Papa's father Pavel - a frustrated musician – abandoned his family to study the violin in St. Petersburg. Papa, a preteen prodigy enrolled in the Moscow Conservatory, supported his family by playing the cello in silent movie theaters, cafés, and even in the lobby of a bordello. Trouble brewed when Pavel returned and reclaimed his position as head of the family. Papa, resentful, ran away on a snowy night taking only his cello. The impetus was partly pride: Pavel had allowed Nadja, Papa's older sister, to marry an arrogant, brutish boy from an alcoholic family over Papa's veto. Apparently Papa's mother had little say in the matter. I can hear Papa's strong voice in my mind. "Absolutely no, Nadja! He's rotten to the core. He'll beat you. I *forbid* you to marry him!" Knowing Papa, it wouldn't have been a veto; it would have been an order. Imagine, Papa, a kid, as the breadwinner and decision-maker in the family.

A kind shopkeeper, Shutkin, rescued Papa and his cello from under a mound of snow the evening he left home and cared for him. Papa never returned to his family, despite that Shutkin lived nearby and his siblings (but not his parents) urged him to come back. After some months, Shutkin died of injuries following a bar room brawl, and Papa set out on his own, as a child in a man's world. Due to prodigious musical talent and resilience, he soon became principal cellist for Moscow's Bolshoi Theater. Later, still a teenager, he played for Lenin as a member of the most famous quartet in Russia. One night in 1921 in the aftermath of the Bolshevik Revolution, he escaped from the Soviet Union, played the cello in odd jobs to survive in Poland, and then crossed into Germany. After hearing Papa play, Wilhelm Furtwängler, the famed conductor of the Berlin Philharmonic, hired Papa as first cellist. Papa, in his early twenties at most, skyrocketed as a soloist thereafter.

In Germany, Papa received a Nansen Certificate of Identity, which was given to lucky European refugees (often Russians) by the League of Nations. This certificate enabled him to visit different countries to perform concerts. But a "Nansen Passport" didn't signify citizenship. Papa, although a celebrity, had no roots or home he could call his own. He existed in a borderless world, a phantom citizen, belonging nowhere, and concertizing everywhere.

Papa dodged pogroms and navigated a dangerous world on his own, while Mama was nurtured in the palaces of Paris.

My childhood memories of Papa in Paris are faint. Although he was an admired son-in-law – a handsome, charismatic celebrity and great musician – I sensed that he often felt like a poor relative who made good – a respected musician, but not an intimate, full Rothschild family member. Later in life Papa admitted to me that he had often felt separate – like a man whose clothes didn't fit quite properly because they were bought ready-made rather than custom-tailored. Historically, musicians came in through the back as paid entertainers, not social equals, no doubt a sensitive issue for him in view of his earlier history. Despite Papa's insecurities, he always charmed everyone, held them spellbound as a raconteur and won them over with his charisma and music. Among his in-laws, Papa felt closest to Babushka. He spent long hours talking to her, especially when she visited us in Los Angeles years later. She loved to play the piano, and he encouraged her to write a book about the composer Luigi Boccherini. Her book, *Luigi Boccherini: His Life and Work*, became an important reference to the little-known Boccherini at that time. *(5)*

I can understand if Papa had felt apart from his in-laws despite being liked and admired by them. The Rothschilds were a clannish family that had amassed a fortune by interacting with one another across European borders (Germany, Austria, France, England and Italy). Even their marriages were frequently between blood relatives. My great-great-grandfather, James de Rothschild, married his niece, Betty, the daughter of his brother Salomon from the Austrian branch of the family. James' son, Alphonse de Rothschild, my great grandfather, married Leonora, a cousin from the English branch of the family. Shared genes had precedence in the Rothschild dynasty, and inheritance favored men over women. *(3)*

I wonder today, did anyone in Mama's family feel vulnerable in Papa's presence, as he had in theirs? This thought never crossed my mind as a boy. Or, much later, did any of my French relatives feel a tinge of vulnerability in my presence – the American maverick, a scientist in the powerful new world, the son of their escaped relative Jacqueline, who succeeded in the foreign land of America on her own?

In addition to genes and a last name, Papa and I shared being Jews. In Papa's case, this meant surviving pogroms and anti-Semitism so flagrant that his family converted to Christianity as a crutch for survival. Papa converted back to Judaism when he left Russia, and always generously supported Israel, especially by concertizing, but he was not religiously observant in childhood or as an adult. Thus, he gave me an ethnic, rather than religious sense, of Judaism.

Mama stamped me a Jew from birth by her Rothschild name alone, which symbolized a Jewish success story – from the ghetto to palaces and princes. Her family honored the high holy days and some Jewish traditions, but I believe religious observances were limited. She told me she even celebrated Christmas with a tree and gifts. I was not an observant Jew. I never had a Bar Mitzvah, didn't learn Hebrew and (almost) never attended services. We celebrated Christmas with a tree and presents, as Mama did, when I was a boy, and sang Christmas carols at a Quaker school in Philadelphia, where we went after Elizabethtown when Papa taught at Curtis Institute of Music.

Although I was raised as a non-observant Jew, we remained keenly aware that we narrowly escaped the crematoriums of the Holocaust. We were concerned that the danger of anti-Semitism could recur at any time and were anxious when we went through customs entering America, due to historical imprints in our psyche. I felt pressure to excel at whatever I did in order to live up to the Jewish tradition of excellence and to be an exemplary model of humanity – generous, polite, modest – to protect myself from anti-Semitism and be a worthy representative of Jews. Being an assimilated Jew and not observing Jewish traditions added to the complexity of my European/American identity.

Although my French and Russian heritages were completely different, they both had origins in Jewish ghettos and achieved extraordinary ascents beyond expectations. Formidable art and virtuoso music were the fabric of my youth; mediocrity was a stranger. Art was valued above all else by my family. The highest rungs of a ladder, defined by excellence, molded my expectations from early childhood. Although secure by inheritance from Mama, I was also driven to match the self-made achievements exemplified by Papa but haunted how to do that.

Papa's family in Russia in front of Papa's home in Ekaterinoslav near the Dneiper River. Papa is sitting in the front row, hands folded, to the right of the very young boy being held by his sister. Papa 's father is the tall, well-dressed man, back row, right. Papa's mother is standing in the back row in the middle of the doorway. The boy in front of Papa's father (row 2, right) is my father's brother Leonid, who became a conductor, with his arms around Shura, who became a cellist, circa 1910.

Papa in Russia, circa 1920.

Windy Cliff camp in the Adirondacks in Elizabethtown, New York,
where I was born in 1940.

Papa's parents, Pavel and Maria, in Russia, circa 1900.

Plastic Elephants

I knew my French family since childhood in America during the war and later in my numerous visits to France, but I had no direct contact with Papa's Russian family as I grew up. I had never met my Russian relatives until I was in college. Papa rarely mentioned his family. Perhaps he was protecting himself, as well as us, by severing memories of his difficult childhood.

I first met my Russian family when I accompanied my parents to Moscow in 1962. Papa was a judge at the Tchaikovsky Music Competition. I was on semester break during my senior year at Harvard. The State Department had bungled the paperwork for our trip, sending me on official business and Papa, the invited celebrity, as my guest. Somehow it got straightened out.

The Cold War was in full effect, and being behind the Iron Curtain a few years after Sputnik had shattered the space barrier, disquieting. The tension between the capitalist United States and communist Soviet Union was palpable, meaning it was scary. We hesitated to say anything out loud in the Soviet Union that could be considered detrimental for fear of being overheard and getting into trouble, whatever that meant, or endangering Papa's family in Moscow. The fact that Papa had married a capitalist Rothschild had not escaped us either. Sometimes fear exists because of known dangers, such as pogroms when Papa was young; our anxiety in Moscow was the uncertainty of danger. Even when my parents and I were alone in our room in the Metropol Hotel we spoke guardedly, assuming our suite was bugged.

Were we VIPs to be handled with soft gloves, or were we adversaries from the West? Who were we?

When our plane had landed at the Moscow airport the Soviet press met us – cameras clicking. It was Papa's first return to his homeland, which was then the Soviet Union, since his escape in 1921. Apparently, he'd been blacklisted when he left the country and married a Rothschild, but he was an honored guest now, a newsworthy celebrity. Changes can be dramatic in a lifetime.

"Greenia!" I heard from a man rushing toward my father.

Greenia? I wondered. Perhaps I'd misheard him.

"They used to call me that at home, as a kid," said Papa.

Perhaps the man had said "Grisha," Papa's nickname for Gregory, which he'd shortened to Gregor, but I didn't think so. I knew so little about Papa.

That was my first glimpse of Papa's cloudy childhood and my mysterious Russian heritage. But it must have been even more disorienting for Papa to greet Anatole, who turned out to be his brother who was born after Papa left. As a symbol of family unity, Anatole gave me a row of linked plastic elephants glued on a base. I was touched, but he remained a stranger, and I remember feeling uncomfortable in his presence. Yet, he was my uncle Anatole, who fit into Papa's family tradition of music by playing the accordion.

Anatole had a 14-year-old son named Gregory (nicknamed Grisha, as Papa). Grisha proudly displayed a Sputnik pin on his shirt when I met him. Many years later he immigrated to New Jersey with his wife, Yelena, and two sons, Misha and Lev. Today, Misha continues the musical lineage as an award-winning jazz pianist in New York. Neither my uncle Anatole nor my cousin Grisha spoke English when I was in Moscow, and I didn't speak Russian, so we stared a lot at one another self-consciously, smiled and made gestures like two chimpanzees.

Meeting his family again after some fifty years was bittersweet for Papa. He had wanted desperately to see his mother, Maria, again. However, he was crushed when he learned during a concert tour in Asia a couple of months earlier that she had died, leaving a void in his heart. Papa had told me that she was kind, intelligent, but uneducated, even illiterate. I presume that he wanted to tell her that he loved her, to apologize for never having returned to see her after he left his family as a little boy, and to assure her that she had never left his thoughts. I'm guessing. He never spoke of tenderness towards his family, or of feeling guilty for not having returned to see them until now. I don't think that he did feel guilty. I'm not even certain that the limited amount Papa did tell me about his family was entirely reliable. What he remembered was a child's impression. For example, my cousin Grisha, now living in New Jersey, told me that Papa's mother read stories to him. That's hardly being illiterate.

The fine line between fact and story blurs as easily as memory fades.

Papa's mother remains an abstraction for me, a person who apparently could read, but perhaps not well, or possibly not at all. She was my grandmother I never met, who spoke a language I didn't understand, and lived in a foreign land considered an adversary in my country.

Papa's father, Pavel, was a shriveled old man when we visited Moscow, but still healthy and the proud possessor of a full mop of hair. He had just remarried after Papa's mother passed away. Papa said the new wife was a shrewish lady. I don't remember meeting her, but maybe I did. Since my grandfather spoke no English, my brief meeting with him amounted to a few nods and a sea of distance between us. Papa insinuated later that he would have preferred not to see his father again as a diminished, provincial, old hen-pecked man. Regardless of what one thinks, parents sit on a private pedestal that is best not toppled.

I also met my uncle Leonid, Papa's oldest brother, in Moscow. Leonid had an amputated foot due to diabetes and wore a prosthetic foot that Papa had sent him from California. He was a tall, childless man – a conductor – but I can't remember of which orchestra. I also can't remember if he was married, divorced or a widower. I know I didn't meet a spouse. It's still so murky for me. I also met uncle Alexander – Shura for short – a musicologist and cellist who had changed his name to Stogorsky to avoid being considered "the lesser Piatigorsky cellist." Shura had a wife and daughter, neither of whom I met. Shura visited Lona and me in Bethesda for a few days many years later. We still couldn't communicate: language again. Overweight Pauline, one of Papa's two sisters, was an expressionless woman, the type one ignores on a bus.

And Papa's sister Nadja, the one who married the boy downstairs against his wishes – where was she?

"Gone," Papa said. "Maybe Siberia."

If I had spoken Russian I would have seen and remembered entirely different people, complex relatives rather than caricatures, for all people are complex and interesting if one speaks their language and understands their culture.

The Soviet Union at the time of my visit was an unhappy place. The airport was deserted and there were few cars in the streets. Our guide seemed terrified to drive by the Kremlin, but I had no idea why. When I paid a few rubles for a small lacquered box I bought from someone in the street, the worried-looking vendor hid behind a tree, scared to be seen accepting money from a tourist, which was illegal. There were special shops strictly for tourists that Russians were not allowed to use. I had no idea that he would be punished, or how severely, if caught selling to a tourist. I slipped him the rubles inconspicuously.

Especially difficult for me was when I had a bout of prostatitis in Moscow. My uncle Shura took me to a local doctor. I waited in a dingy basement filled with expressionless, downtrodden looking patients. Eventually I was treated with a catheter containing antibiotics (so they claimed) in a small bathroom, an experience that seemed straight out of a novel by Dostoevsky. Our Russian guide was horrified when he heard that I had gone to a local doctor and immediately made arrangements for me to see a doctor for tourists in a respectable, clean medical facility.

That evening I saw the ballet *Giselle* at the Bolshoi Theater. What a contrast! The setting, music, dancing and enthusiastic audience were unforgettable and mesmerizing. That was a Russian heritage to be proud of, especially with Papa having been its principal cellist many years ago. But even the famous Bolshoi performing a western ballet was set in a world apart from mine. The audience clapped in unison, joining the many to one. It seemed to my American standards, which stress individualism, more like an army on parade than spectators engrossed in art.

Earlier in the week, Papa had visited the Bolshoi orchestra and was struck by the stagnation. "Nothing has changed," he said in amazement. "The room and the sheets of music still have my handwritten name on them."

Imagine! Sheets of music with adolescent Papa's handwritten name were still being used in the Bolshoi Theater fifty years later.

The Soviet Union in the 1960s was foreign territory where I was out of place. I felt like a wealthy American, not a poor American, as I'd felt in France, nor as a wealthy Frenchman, as I'd felt in America. I certainly didn't feel Russian. My Russian kin were strangers, despite my Russian genes and Russian name.

We are all children of our parents. We carry their genes and are exposed to their values, as our parents are children of their parents, and so on up the line. We adapt as evolving species do in new niches by exploiting mutations within inherited genes.

In Moscow at the Tchaikovsky Music Competition with Papa's cello student Douglas Davis on my right, 1962.

My uncle Anatole (Papa's brother) and I in Moscow when I accompanied
my parents at the Tchaikovsky Music Competition, 1962.

Shura (Alexander Stogorsky, Papa's brother) playing the cello, circa 1960s.

Jephta (left) and I (right) flanking my uncle Shura (Papa's brother) visiting from the Soviet Union at my home in Bethesda. circa 1980s.

Mama and Papa playing music together in Elizabethtown, circa 1943.

Light from Darkness

My parents had neither exposure to science nor any notion of what a scientist actually did. We never discussed scientific developments at dinner or anywhere else because we didn't know anything about it. Science didn't occupy any space in my family. I never played with chemistry or erector sets, or tinkered with the mechanisms of watches, or assembled short wave radios. I didn't read science magazines, as most adolescent boys interested in science would.

I labored through inorganic chemistry, which was the only science course given at my high school. Math frustrated me. Plane geometry was bad enough, but solid geometry was a catastrophe. I struggled to visualize three-dimensional shapes and found it much easier to think conceptually than structurally. I loved ideas. Jephta was the math wizard (majoring in math at college), and I relied on her, and sometimes on Mama, for help with homework. Papa was the only person I ever met who was worse at math than I was.

Fish were the first sign of my future involvement with science. I filled my bedroom with tanks of freshwater tropical fish I bought from the pet store and bred the livebearers (guppies, platys, swordtails). I marveled at the diverse, colorful species (hatchet fish, neon tetras, angelfish), but this was more an aesthetic than scientific hobby.

Mama strangely assumed I would be a scientist. In part I believe she wanted to protect me from being compared with my famous cellist father, although she correctly recognized that I had little musical talent. But Mama admired scientists, or at least her unformed notion of a scientist. She kept a couple of old chemistry scales on a shelf but never used them. It's interesting how objects inconspicuously lying here and there often reflect hidden interests of their owners.

Unlike the French Rothschilds, who focused on art and banking, the English branch of the family made a significant mark in science in addition to art collecting, banking and serving as members of parliament, and created massive collections of biological specimens.(6-8) The brothers Charles (1877-1923) and Walter (1868-1937) took an active interest – an obsession may be more accurate – in biology. Walter Rothschild collected hundreds of thousands of bird skins, bird eggs and nests, bird skeletons, beetles, reptiles, mammals and fish, as well as 2.5 million butterflies and moths from many different countries, which formed the basis of his Zoological Museum at Tring that opened in 1892 and operated for forty years. Eventually Walter sold many of his bird skins to the American Museum of Natural History to pay off debts. The rest of Walter's zoological collection landed in the British Natural History Museum after his death.

Walter's brother, Charles, an entomologist as well as a banker and politician, amassed a flea collection of some 260,000 specimens, which also resides in the British Natural History Museum. Charles's daughter, Miriam Lane, was a world authority on fleas, butterflies and chemical communication among insects, and her brother Nathaniel Mayer Victor Rothschild (known as Lord Victor Rothschild), was a noted scientist and science advisor for industry and government.

The Rothschild natural history collections led to the identification of many new species, some of which were named after them. One famous discovery by Charles resulting from collecting in Sudan was the plague vector flea, *Xenopsylla cheopis* (Rothschild), which he described in a 1903 publication.

The Rothschild craze for biology continued with Lionel (often called Mr. Lionel to distinguish him from his grandfather, Baron Lionel), a cousin of Charles and Walter. Mr. Lionel cultivated and collected rhododendrons. Walter and Charles also had their hands in horticulture. Walter concentrated on irises and Charles on orchids. Amschel Rothschild, the eldest son of the original Mayer Amschel of Frankfurt, developed gardens in Frankfurt, and Charlotte, daughter-in-law of Nathan, founder of the English branch, had an extensive orchid collection. (The Rothschilds had the confusing habit of reusing the same names for generations.) Samples of these Rothschild horticultural specimens found homes in the Royal Botanic Gardens, Kew, the Natural History Museum and the Royal Botanic Gardens, Edinburgh.

The Rothschild gardeners, George Reynolds and James Hudson, published numerous articles on the culture and growth of orchids.

Rothschild plant and orchid collecting was no amateur

activity. Delegates of a Royal Horticultural Society conference in 1906 held at Gunnersbury, a Rothschild estate,
spoke of 'genetics', the same year that the English scientist,
William Bateson, coined the term 'genetics' to initiate a new
field of physiology. This was three years before Wilhelm
Johannsen came up with the term 'gene', which remains the
backbone of biology.

Mama never spoke of this rich tradition of biology and
science in the English branch of the Rothschilds, and I'm
uncertain how much she even knew about it. It was never
brought to my attention as I was growing up, though much
later I did know Miriam Lane and her brother, Lord Victor,
both accomplished scientists.

The slight exposure to science from family that I had as
a boy came from Mama's sister, Bethsabée. She received a
bachelor's degree in biology at the Sorbonne in Paris and
studied biochemistry and biology at Columbia University in
New York, but she never received an advanced degree. She
established The Batsheva de Rothschild Science Fund
(Bethsabée became Batsheva when she moved to Israel) that
sponsored international seminars in various topics in basic
and medical science of special interest to Israel and provided
small grants to support research of young Israeli scientists.
Bethsabée's main interest, however, was sponsoring modern
dance. She befriended and supported the American modern
dancer, Martha Graham, and created the Batsheva Dance
Company in Israel that still exists today. (I was honored
to ballroom dance with Martha Graham once at my sister's

wedding, which apparently was extremely rare for her. I told her she danced well!). Later, Bethsabée created a second dance company in Israel, the Bat Dor Dance Company, for Jeannette Rodman, an immigrant from South Africa. Dance, not science, was Bethsabée's love and major preoccupation. So, even my aunt, as scientifically bent as she was, concentrated in sponsoring art.

Papa talked romantically about nature, especially about oceanography. He was convinced that the oceans were the wave of the future. He often told me, "We know almost nothing about the oceans, yet oceans comprise most of our planet." He never mentioned currents or salinity or the physics of waves, and he knew little about marine life. He thought eels went to a special burial ground to die and wondered where that was, and he talked about great battles between giant squids and sperm whales in the depth of the seas. He was attracted to jungles and fascinated by snakes, but these, too, were fantasies. Once he went for an overnight camping trip in the desert with a herpetology professor and came home excited about how they had caught a snake. That was the sum of his experiences in science, as far as I'm aware. I disappointed him when I didn't keep a king snake that I received as a gift from a friend of his. The idea of feeding it live mice, as recommended, repulsed me.

If I had been asked how I imagined science when I set my sights on becoming a scientist, I wouldn't have mentioned research to cure diseases, or to combat pollution with new energy sources, or to improve agricultural methods to feed growing populations in developing countries, or to discover the origin of life or the universe. I would have imagined whales fighting with giant squids, or jellyfish bursting from the deep like translucent, living pieces of jewelry, or adventures exploring new species in the Arctic or desert or jungle. I was drawn to the abstraction of science as influenced by Papa's fantasies, Mama's intuition and my own musings. Thus, before I knew anything about science, it loomed as mystery and beauty, a view that has never completely left me.

Even when I was a fully engaged scientist, science remained tinged with magic. When I peered at the clear night sky, I thought of space, time and black holes, but at the same time I fixed my gaze on stars that sparkled as if within reach, belying that their light had traveled unimaginable distances even after they had been extinguished millions, if not billions, of years ago. Unreachable dead stars that danced before my eyes – light from darkness – so remarkable that it bordered on fantasy. That was magic.

I must have unwittingly projected the image of a romantic marine scientist to my classmates in high school, since my senior yearbook foreshadowed me as a famous oceanographer living on a yacht on the Mediterranean Sea. This projection was not of a scientist analyzing diagrams, innovating technology or curing diseases. It was of a scientist traveling the oceans in luxury, more a gentleman than a scientist.

But childhood predictions are hardly credible. My true path in science was a bumpier and less luxurious adventure.

I'm the boy in a tie on the top left of the Jungle Jim in kindergarten in Friends Select School in Philadelphia.

Jephta and I piloting over Paris, circa 1950.

Jephta and I dressed for a fancy occasion, circa 1948.

Tough guy getting ready for life, circa 1952.

My second-grade class at Friends Select School, Philadelphia. I'm in a coat and tie, looking lost, on the extreme right of the second row, 1947.

High school graduation reception at Black-Foxe Military Academy with Papa and Jephta on my right and Mama on my left, 1958.

The Idea of Science

If scientists are supposed to be "brainy" (a term requiring a liberal definition!), an IQ test I took at the beginning of high school didn't bode well for my future in science.

"Were you feeling all right?" my teacher asked the week after I took the exam. He must have expected more from me since I was the top student in my class of seventeen.

"Well, I did have a cold that day," I said.

"Aha! I thought there was an explanation," he replied. "I would like you to retake the exam."

I did, the following day, in the Principal's office. I was told there would be no distractions there. He didn't consider my fear of sitting alone in the principal's office retaking the IQ exam that I had presumably "flunked" the first time around a distraction. Despite inquiries, I was never told the results of my first or second IQ test.

"We don't want Joram to develop an inferiority complex," they said.

Considerate.

On the positive side, never knowing my IQ allowed me to flap my wings and hope I would fly. To this day my IQ remains fluttering in the vast blue sky, and that's where it should remain. When others boast of their IQ, I remain silent, pleased that this measure of intelligence is outdated.

The mandatory college entrance exams – those nasty Scholastic Aptitude Tests – were another nightmare. Sample tests I took showed that I needed improvement to be accepted in a college of my choice. To boost my score in English, I memorized over the two-week Christmas break from school definitions of words listed alphabetically in the practice booklet. I ran out of steam by the time I got to the words starting with the letter m. Nonetheless, my efforts were sufficient to raise my SAT score considerably; my math score remained somewhere in the middle range. What a ridiculous measure of ability to do well in college, or anywhere else.

Miraculously, I got into Harvard. I doubt that my Scholastic Aptitude Test results had much to do with that, but at least they didn't automatically exclude me. Possible reasons for being accepted were that my Rothschild heritage promised future financial contributions, that my father was a famous cellist, that I was a highly ranked junior tennis player in Southern California (I had a mean left-handed serve), and that I was academically first in my (tiny) class (of seventeen) at Black-Foxe Military Academy. Finally, I was from Los Angeles, which probably added geographic diversity to Harvard's student body in Boston, an euphemism that I understand was also applicable in the 1950s for maintaining a Jewish quota, although that might have been less strict at Harvard than other colleges.

Soon after I arrived at Harvard I took aptitude tests given to freshmen for guidance towards a major field of study. More testing for ability! I remember staring at graphs with the clock ticking in my head – quickly, quickly, time's running out – not sure exactly which of the multiple choices were correct. Was this what science was all about? Was this the measure of my ability to be a scientist – graphs and numbers and a ticking clock?

A few weeks later I received a thin envelope with a letter saying, "Not much gift for the natural sciences...SocRel best hope for reaching Dean's List...good luck."

No gift for natural sciences! SocRel? What was that? The grapevine said it was a watered-down mixture of sociology and psychology. Really?

I crumpled the letter and aimed for the trash.

This was one of those rare moments from long ago that stood out, and it said, "Abandon your life's plan. You won't succeed." In truth, I did struggle with math and graphs, and I didn't like the laboratory part of the chemistry course I took in high school. My desire to become a scientist had been driven by the imaginative yet uninformed views of my parents, especially Papa. Perhaps it was only the idea of becoming a scientist that attracted me. But, I believe I would have lost self-esteem if I had dropped my goal in science to follow impersonal advice derived from a standardized test. I had become wary of standardized tests, even if it was reflexive self-protection against poor performances.

Should I admit defeat before the battle even started? What to believe or choose as a major? Science, SocRel, some other subject? Which one? Was ignoring advice idiotic, foolishly stubborn and arrogant?

I pondered the idea of science, not whether I had talent to be a scientist. For me, science was the beauty of nature, which was an abstraction. I doubt I could have defined exactly what that meant for me. What was important was that before I'd taken a single science course at college, I thought of science poetically – science as fantasy – not as a discipline driven by curiosity or a method to achieve a goal, such as curing disease. Also, I had the distinct advantage of financial independence in choosing a profession, so I didn't consider science as a source of income. I remember trusting my intuition, the message from my heart, regardless of my ignorance. I never really considered doing anything else but science, not then, not ever.

My thoughts turned to advice that Papa had received as a young music student in Russia from Mr. Kinkulkin, a professional cellist, recounted in his autobiography, *Cellist*:

"While I played, Mr. Kinkulkin tapped his tiny fingers on a table and cleaned his nails with a toothpick. He remained silent until I had put my cello away. 'Listen carefully, my boy. Tell your father that I strongly advise you to choose a profession that will suit you. Keep away from the cello. You have no talent whatsoever'." *(4)*

What a shock that must have been to Papa, an infinitely gifted boy with his heart set on being a cellist, dismissed as talentless with no future in his dreams. He didn't even have the benefit of being directed to another career, a SocRel equivalent. He quit the cello for a short stint after being put down by Kinkulkin, but not for long fortunately.

In a leap of faith based on the cliché that the apple doesn't fall far from the tree, I interpreted the unfavorable evaluation of my science aptitude as destiny to future success in science. With such ungrounded optimism, I majored in biology and never looked back. My disregarding the results of aptitude tests and opinions of outside "experts" initiated a lifelong pattern of questioning authorities and the need to prove myself.

It was my first stab at transforming a demon of doubt into an angel of advantage.

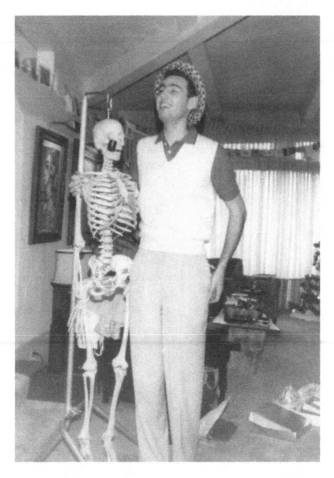

A light moment embracing a model skeleton smoking Papa's pipe in Los Angeles, circa 1960.

Papa and I together at home in Los Angeles, 1963.

The Speed of Dark

Although hopeful I'd made the right decision to major in biology, family demons pecked at me like angry chickens.

First was the challenge of living up to the standards of my illustrious father, which seemed insurmountable. I consistently was asked, "Are you related to the musician, *the* famous cellist?"

"Yes," I said. And then suddenly I became an interesting person.

"Do you play an instrument?"

"No."

"Really? Why not?"

There was no single answer to that question. I lacked musical talent, my home was not a good place to play badly, I had other interests, and so forth.

The most blatant question I was ever asked was, "Are you a failure like the sons of all great men?"

We had just met at a social occasion and sipping drinks. Was she joking? Not according to her expression.

"Not yet," I said, tightening the grip on my glass, hoping (unsuccessfully) to deflect her with humor. I was a young scientist at the time, and she was neither the first nor the last to have touched a vulnerable nerve of being recognized in my father's shadow.

I was proud of Papa, of course, but the demon whispered in my ear relentlessly, "Yes, Joram, you are related, you are an authentic Piatigorsky...but the son."

How to shine my own light in a way that would satisfy me and not be obscured by Papa's brilliant glare? My life couldn't have been more different than Papa's, who had withstood pogroms and poverty, lacked formal education (except for music), ran away from home as a child, escaped revolutions and wars, and rose to international stardom before his twenties.

I was an American citizen in a peaceful country, financially secure, pampered by loving parents, surrounded with great art, and educated with peers in fine schools. How could anyone compare me with Papa? But, he was my father, and I did feel the weight of comparison.

So here I was, eighteen years old at prestigious Harvard, planning a career in science and confronted by daunting academic challenges. I had the finest professors – Louis Fieser for organic chemistry, B. F. Skinner for psychology, Konrad Bloch for biochemistry (he was awarded the Nobel Prize the day he gave his first lecture in the course) and many other prominent scholars – creating a landscape of academic splendor.

I loved my science courses – each scientific fact was a new gem added to my growing collection of facts. However, I struggled with some of the concepts. I had a hard time grasping how adenosine triphosphate (ATP) stored and released energy to drive biochemistry within the cell. What exactly was energy? How does breaking a phosphate chemical bond release energy for use? One cold evening, I biked over to the labs to ask my teaching assistant, a graduate student, to explain energy and ATP. Although he patiently answered my questions, and I appreciated the complexity of science, I still struggled to understand the relationship between energy and a biochemical bond. I worried that the aptitude tests were right about my lacking talent for science, and often questioned whether I was really destined for a career in science. Apparently, that teaching assistant also questioned my future in science. We met again a few years later by chance in Puget Sound when I was a graduate student at Caltech, and he said, "Oh, Joram, I'm relieved to see you're doing well in science. I was worried about you."

So was I, but I kept that to myself.

I found science especially exciting when it spoke to me in artistic terms. I was sold from day one in the course on comparative anatomy. The professor, Alfred Romer, sat on the desk in front of the class, his legs dangling above the floor, and sang, "It's a long way from amphioxus." I joined the class applause. Later I heard that he was famous for this performance. Romer's masterful lectures on the reptilian jawbone evolving into the mammalian middle ear bones, whetted my appetite for evolution, and in those early days it traveled from my ear to my heart. Here was science presented as both observation and narrative, each reinforcing the other without equations or abstractions. But it wasn't all sweet harmony. There were the weekly comparative anatomy labs where we dissected frogs and other animals to learn how vertebrates were constructed, which required memorizing innumerable anatomical details. Working through the pungent smell of formaldehyde added to the strain.

I thought I was doing okay until my lab partner, a woman who looked frustrated every time I asked her how to locate a nerve or vein, said in a somber tone, "This isn't going to work, Joram. I plan to get into med school here and you're holding me back. I've got to ace this course. You're on your own."

Whoa! I certainly didn't want to ruin her career. So then I was on my own, cutting up corpses and memorizing the names of ligaments, tendons, muscles, bones of different species. I ended up enjoying working solo. Sam and Marcia, lab partners who sat next to me, befriended me, a benefit of having been dumped. They married after college and we stayed in touch for some fifty years.

As for my ex-partner, I heard when I was a graduate student that she was still on track to get into medical school.

It wasn't only the complex anatomy of vertebrates that I learned to appreciate in college. A course in physiology opened my eyes to the biochemical balance of life. I remember conducting experiments on the beating heart of a decapitated turtle. As remarkable as heart physiology was, the ability of the headless turtle to stay "alive" for hours impressed me even more. Why didn't the turtle die without a head, like the poor victims of the guillotine in the French Revolution? What did life mean, and how did life differ, if at all, in different species? What might we learn about life from other species that few pay any attention to?

I was most impressed with invertebrates – worms, snails, crabs, sea anemones and the like, quite an extensive list of species. Unlike vertebrates, which had more similarities than differences, the colorful invertebrates epitomized diversity. Some even resembled plants more than animals, and the developing larvae of some looked nothing like their mature form. No generality applied. As a group, invertebrates were a basketful of gems. I was drawn to their diversity – they raised endless questions about their evolution and biology, yet relatively few scientists seemed to study them.

Everything I learned about invertebrates in college – from the lowly sponge to the sophisticated octopus – was new and surprising. They were an alternate world filled with wonder. That so many people considered these beautiful, exquisitely adapted animals to be no more than squishy nuisances, attracted me even more.

I also loved literature courses. Shakespeare's conversion of history into stories about human conflict fascinated me, and I read passages over and over for the sheer beauty of the language. I learned how great writers such as Moliere and Rabelais and Cervantes and many others transformed observations on society and behavior into imaginative and often comic narratives. The science and literature courses at Harvard sowed dormant seeds in my mind that sprouted slowly in my career.

As essential as formal education was for becoming a scientist, however, I didn't want to rely on academic institutions as my platform. A private conversation I overheard between two students touched on the absurdity, in my view, of connecting an institution with self-worth.

One said to the other, "When I was in high school, I was valedictorian and thought I was a genius. Then Harvard accepted me, which confirmed it. When I got here, though, everyone else was a valedictorian, and I wasn't so special or sure anymore."

"I know what you mean," said the other. "But, I don't know, in my case, I'm not convinced yet."

I wondered if he meant that he wasn't convinced whether being at Harvard made him a genius, or whether he was a genius with or without Harvard? Never mind!

Papa's shadow of the self-made man hovered over me. I was privileged to attend Harvard, but it didn't substitute for being successful. Both of my parents stood tall without college degrees. Brought up in the Parisian palaces of the French Rothschilds, notably at a magnificent residence at the Place de la Concorde purchased by James, the first Rothschild to settle in France, Mama received limited home schooling. Girls at the time were not groomed to be professional women. My mother's academic credentials amounted to a high school equivalency diploma she obtained at 28 after immigrating to America, and a few correspondence courses at Temple University in Philadelphia during the war years. Her many accomplishments – author (*Jump in the Waves*), chess patron and   champion inducted into the U.S. Chess Hall of Fame, tennis champion and stone sculptor, as well as amateur musician (pianist, bassoonist, and even composer under the pseudonym of Paul Ari) made a poor case for the importance of academic degrees.

Papa's formal schooling amounted to short stints at music conservatories and a few philosophy lectures in

Germany as a young man. Yet he spoke three languages, authored an autobiography (*Cellist*) published in English, which was translated into Japanese, Hungarian and German. He also wrote poetry and a novel he never published. His intelligence and originality, coupled with his celebrity as a cellist, shone brightly. His diplomas were honorary doctorate degrees from prestigious universities.

Papa was his own institution.

In short, the template for success in my family was to rise by one's own ingenuity, and conflicted feelings of the need to "break free" tugged at me. Papa often asked me when I was going "to enter the school of life." Each time I was irritated, but remained silent, thinking, wasn't I doing all right? Nonetheless, I recognized that the question had merit.

"A doctorate degree diminishes the man," Papa said, not completely in jest.

"How so?" I asked, still a student dreaming of my future.

"Well," he asked, "who is more significant, Beethoven or Dr. Beethoven?"

I wondered whether Piatigorsky was as significant as Dr. Piatigorsky.

Despite feeling overcast by Papa's shadow, his achievements gave me confidence that I too could realize my goals, regardless of how I fantasized them. If success was a family trait, if I shared Papa's genes, why should I be excluded? Papa, called a genius by some and admired by all, was still a man, like other men, like me, with foibles as well as strengths. I saw his quirks (unable to prepare a meal, even boil an egg), conflicts (stage fright mixed with confidence, terror of what music critics might write, yet confident he knew best) and weaknesses (a disaster at math, he multiplied by adding long columns of numbers), as much his sterling qualities (virtuoso cellist, beloved teacher, compelling raconteur and writer). This human perspective cast a softer hue and made his high status seem less godly, and blended certainty with doubt in one package.

"Focus on your strengths," Papa told me over and over again. "Everyone knows their weaknesses. The strengths are harder to identify. Know your strengths."

This simple message – focus on my strengths – helped me step out of Papa's shadow. I needed to find my strengths and harness them, not dwell on weaknesses. While this at times promoted childish, unrealistic dreams – winning Wimbledon during my teenage tennis days, or receiving accolades as a scientist – I tried to appreciate and develop my strengths rather than struggle to improve my weaknesses.

There was another adage that Papa often repeated: "Stick with the people who pull you up, not those who push you down."

When I asked him how to identify those people, he said what I already knew. Some individuals inspired me and gave me confidence – pulled me up – and some made me feel a little less – pushed me down. It had nothing to do with professional advantages to be gained or lost, or about flatterers: it had everything to do with the personal chemistry within relationships. It was wise advice with broad relevance that I believe helped Papa weave his way through difficult times.

My regret was that I never asked him who it was that pulled him up.

No matter how much I tried, I never succeeded in giving a satisfactory answer to Papa's question, "What exactly are you looking for in your research?" His eyes glazed over whenever I mentioned genes or any other specific aspect of my work. I admit that scientific concepts are foreign without some training; nonetheless, Papa's incomprehension of science left a gap between us. We were a family of artists, not scientists. Years earlier, Papa had imagined science as a romantic adventure. Now, as I was becoming a scientist, I portrayed science as incomprehensible and lacking adventure and charisma. At times he would ask me when I was going to leave the artificial laboratory and go out into nature, which was his version of science. I had no satisfying answer. I never talked to him about the wonder of invertebrates, or how literature seemed to enhance my appreciation of science as narrative. These early impressions needed time to develop and mature. I was still an embryo of my adult form, and what embryo is conscious of the future?

In short, Papa made me feel unappreciated – unable to take a bow or show off a bit for a job well done. Once, he was invited to play a semi-private concert at Caltech for the staff. I sat in the last row of the small auditorium. He played beautifully, as always, and I was proud to be his son. However, Caltech was my territory, yet he made no mention that I was a graduate student there in the audience. After the concert he had no time to visit my laboratory. I felt as if I didn't exist. In some sense, I didn't. On another occasion

Papa visited me in Bethesda when I was a postdoctoral fellow at the National Institutes of Health. I took him to my lab and showed him how I removed the eye lens from a chicken embryo under the dissecting microscope, a delicate process requiring microsurgery. As soon as I cracked open the shell to expose the embryo, he ran out of the lab muttering, "Take it away, take it away; it's so pink!"

He never set foot in my lab again.

In Switzerland a few years later, when he had already been diagnosed with lung cancer, but was still teaching at Montreux in Switzerland, I gave a lecture nearby at the University of Geneva. He said he had a teaching commitment and could not take the afternoon off to hear my talk. I was very disappointed. I missed an opportunity to show myself in a different light, more professional, a promising scientist in a world of my own making. If he had come, it would have been a happy occasion for me, and no doubt an interesting one for him. He died of cancer a year later and never heard me give a science talk.

Life is mixed, however; ups and downs blend in positive and negative ways. I was lucky: I had more ups than downs, and more positives than negatives.

Perhaps the most important positive influence that Papa had on me, which I doubt he realized, was his originality. He was a champion at what I call "mental gymnastics." For example, I remember being home on semester break from college and telling him that nothing can travel faster than the speed of light, a fact I had learned in my physics class.

"Nothing?" he said.

"Nothing," I repeated, confident of my new knowledge.

"What about the speed of dark?" he asked.

A physicist would smile dismissively at such silliness. The "speed of dark" was scientifically ridiculous; there's bright light and dim light. Nonetheless, Papa's way of seeing the world from multiple perspectives, as a gymnast might contort his body, encouraged diverse ways of thinking. He twisted ideas creatively, turned reality upside down despite the risk of being contrary, and had a sense of humor with deeper significance than laughter. Of recent interest, physicists are speculating that the mysterious dark matter of the universe may interact with an undefined "dark" force that is carried by a so-called dark-photon – all speculative, but if there's some truth in this, one might ask, what's the speed of this new "dark light"?

When I have taken contrary positions, or played the devil's advocate, I may have appeared foolish or ignorant, and I often felt I did, but questioning – challenging – common beliefs, even in jest, peering through an unfiltered lens, asking questions because they occurred to me, could be creative and, even unintentionally, hit on a novel insight.

Taking chances, stepping outside the norm, sits at the core of creativity and is at the heart of good science, as long as it is not done for the sake of being different or a rebel. Permission to take chances was an angel in disguise – a special delivery from Papa.

Mama was the polar opposite of Papa for me in numerous ways. She stayed home with Jephta and me while Papa traveled constantly, and consequently I developed a closer relationship with her than with him. She was born in 1911, two years after her older brother Guy, and just ten months after her elder brother, Édouard Alphonse Émile Lionel (called Alphonse), died tragically of appendicitis at the age of four. Her sister Bethsabée, three years younger than Mama, was the baby in the family. Thus, Mama was a "replacement child" for her dead sibling Alphonse, consistent with the "Rothschild, but a Girl" chapter title in her memoir, *Jump in the Waves,* which I realize matches my own demon that I was "Piatigorsky, but the son." *(9)*

I don't know whether Mama's fierce determination to excel was driven by a sense that she needed to replace Alphonse, or whether she was genetically wired for success, or both. She was a strong-willed, intelligent polymath, who I never heard boast or speak highly of herself. If anything, she was insecure. Before going to compete in a chess or tennis tournament, she generally asked me, "Is it okay if I lose?"

"It's okay," I reassured her, but was pretty sure she wouldn't lose.

Her goals were not dreams; they were requirements to prove her worth. She associated failure with shame, and she collected achievements.

Mama saw life as a never-ending series of small obstacles to overcome, one step at a time, always directed to higher levels of achievement. She was extremely ambitious, without admitting it openly, and possibly without even realizing it. This sent me a double-sided message. One side encouraged gradual, attainable steps toward accomplishments; the other applied constant pressure to take another step, and then another, relentlessly marching towards a higher level of achievement. If I received a C at school, rather than criticize, she would praise me if I got a C + the following semester, and then more praise for a B after that, and so forth on up. She assumed – guaranteed – that the next step would be achieved, giving me confidence and direction. However, that "guarantee" came at a cost: it made success as mandatory as breathing. Not achieving it meant failure – a shameful situation. There was always another step to take, more to accomplish, further to travel, keeping any final destination perpetually on the horizon, which made it difficult, if not impossible, to satisfy an undefined goal.

Mama's Rothschild wealth bestowed independence, which allowed me to think of science idealistically instead of a means of support. However, that gift was not without strings. I feared being set apart from my peers. I was self-conscious of appearing spoiled or privileged, of being branded "rich," which meant what? That I had an easier professional road, a privileged path, or that I was lazy and considered science a hobby rather than a substantive career?

Monetary gains, a major incentive and mark of success for most people, didn't provide the same satisfaction as recognition and professional advancement for me. I didn't associate more money with accomplishment or pride, which stole one of the major marks of success in our culture.

Therefore, I kept my Rothschild heritage quiet and blushed if it was mentioned in public. I wanted to be considered equal with friends and colleagues, not separate. I parked my red Mercedes 190 SL sports car, a gift from Papa, several blocks from my laboratory at Caltech, because I was afraid it was too ostentatious. There was a tacit honor among students – a certificate of membership – in driving a beat-up jalopy or living on the edge. How often we celebrate the impoverished immigrant who rises to towering heights. We were immigrants, but hardly impoverished.

I hesitated inviting anyone to my home when I was a student, as well as throughout much of my adulthood, because it might appear too fancy with all the art. I also worried that gifts I gave would seem too expensive, yet I didn't want to appear cheap. I remember my chagrin when, still a graduate student, I gave a postdoctoral fellow in the laboratory a stereo set as a gift.

"My goodness, Joram. I can't accept this."

"Why not? I have another stereo and am not using this. I thought you wanted one."

"Yes, well no. It's too much," he said.

He was adamant. I took it back, feeling very self-conscious. Was it really too much?

But I don't mean to imply that I didn't appreciate wealth from Mama. Rather than diverting me from science or serious personal effort, financial security drove me to work harder to prove that my worth was not my bank account. And especially important, being raised with financial security punctured the myth – often a stigma – that money spoils. Money is an indispensable commodity, not a human value. Money doesn't spoil or produce anything on its own. My parents taught me this by example, not by artificially withholding or feigning the truth of our finances.

My challenge, then, on my path to becoming a scientist was to live up to the standards of my unique, gifted European parents, despite being a native-born, formally educated, wealthy American blessed with a surplus of advantages. 'Privileged boy makes good' hardly deserves headlines, and positive headlines were plentiful in my family. I needed to clear the high bar set by my unusual family.

Mama, an award-winning, bronze medalist in the 1957 chess Olympics, and chess patron, landed her in the United States Chess Hall of Fame posthumously in 2014.

Jephta, my parents and I watching a tennis match, circa 1953.

My parents playing chess on a portable chess set, circa 1950s.

I caught a weird looking fish with Papa in Coronado, California, 1955.

Drawn to the Sea

The summer of 1960 following my sophomore year at college I was an intern under the umbrella of Boyd W. Walker, a professor of marine fish in the Department of Zoology at the University of California at Los Angeles (UCLA). My first task consisted of topping off partly filled bottles containing fish fixed in formaldehyde. The bottles on dusty shelves in a dark room reeked of insignificance. Many of the fish were new species discovered each time the research vessel went on a collecting trip. My first thought was whether I'd have a chance to go out on one of those trips.

I never did.

After a few weeks, Arthur Myrberg, a PhD graduate student working for Walker, took pity on me, woozy from the smell of alcohol mixed with formaldehyde.

"Would you be interested in assisting my doctorate research?" he asked.

"Would I? Yes!"

This was my entry into scientific research: an opportunity because I was at the right place at the right time. The project concerned imprinting in cichlid fish called "Kissing" Gouramis and Angel fish, the same species I had when I was a teenager. I sat in a darkened laboratory (so as not to disturb them) and recorded their behavior to see if they would care for their own young but eat those of other species. Although I made no conclusive observations, I became curious about animal behavior. Also, I remember my satisfaction in studying problems that very few scientists even knew existed.

This work intrigued me enough to consider a career studying the brain and led to my taking a course at Harvard on the neurophysiological basis of behavior and another on the determination of human behavior by the famed B. F. Skinner. I visited Nikolaas Tinbergen (who shared the 1973 Nobel Prize with Lorenz in Medicine and Physiology) at Oxford University to explore the possibility of doing graduate work in animal behavior. My naïve idea was to determine what happens in the brain at the moment a thought or an epiphany or a forgotten name at the tip of one's tongue suddenly flashes in mind – the "a-ha" moment – the brain equivalent of an epiphany that makes one exclaim, "Oh yes, I remember," or, "I get it." Ultimately, I did not follow the neurophysiological route. I believed that our ability to understand the biochemistry or biophysics or nerve wiring diagram, or whatever happened in the brain, was a research topic for my children or grandchildren. Science was not at the stage yet to make sense of it all. But the topic – the biology of a thought or an epiphany – was fascinating to me, and still is.

As an aside, it is only now, more than fifty years later, that research is finally connecting epiphany with brain activity. There's a *New York Times* article by John Kounis, who states "eureka moments are associated with a distinctive burst of high-frequency activity in the brain's right temporal lobe. This burst of activity is preceded by a brief 'brain blink' during which a person is momentarily less aware of his or her environment. Neither of these neural patterns is detectable when a person solves a problem analytically."

After my junior year at college, I asked my distant cousin, Lord Victor Rothschild, a British biologist at Cambridge University, if he could help me find a summer job in science in England. He put me in touch with Harold Barnes, a scientist who investigated barnacles at the University Marine Biological Station Millport, on the island of Great Cumbrae in the Firth of Clyde, Scotland, run by the University of London. This kindled my sense of adventure: science on a remote island! Barnes wanted a summer intern who knew about spectroscopy.

"No problem," I said, and then I looked up spectroscopy. I barely knew how to spell it. It turned out that all Barnes needed was a student willing to spend hours measuring colorimetric reactions using a spectrophotometer, a rote process that required more patience than expertise.

For approximately a month that summer I performed experiments to determine how long a barnacle (a shrimp-like crustacean enclosed upside-down in a shell) that is underwater at high tide and exposed to air at low tide could survive without being immersed in oxygen-containing sea water. I measured the accumulation of lactic acid, a product of metabolism without oxygen, in barnacles kept for increasing time intervals in a nitrogen-saturated atmosphere. In science jargon, how much of an oxygen debt could the intertidal barnacles withstand?

In some experiments I needed to take samples every hour for twenty-four hours. I was grateful for thick wool Scottish sweaters, since I was asked politely to refrain from using the portable electric heater during the chilly nights in order to conserve money. The Scots deserve their reputation for being thrifty. Those long, quiet, lonely nights in the small marine laboratory by the sea were indescribably satisfying and to this day remain a highlight of my career. Publishing, recognitions of various sorts, participating on panels establishing funding and policy, lecturing and teaching are all invaluable parcels of the life of a scientist. But quiet anonymity, isolated from the frantic front, immersed in nature and experimentation – merging into a greater whole, becoming a piece in the puzzle that forms the image – is a supreme privilege of being a research scientist. At the end of my twenty-four-hour marathon experiments, shortly after five in the morning, just after the seagulls began to chatter at the first light of dawn, the custodian arrived to tidy up before the scientists came. We greeted the sunrise together with a biscuit and tea with milk. He insisted on the hot milk. I'm not a tea drinker, but I never had a more welcome breakfast, or met a more contented man.

One experiment in Millport that ended in disaster taught me an important lesson. I dried a series of barnacles overnight, placing each of the 60 samples in a separate pre-weighed bottle in a warm oven. I lined up the bottles sequentially in rows from left to right, as if reading a book. I thought this would save me the trouble of labeling each bottle. What I hadn't appreciated was the slight vibration of the oven. The next morning I found, to my horror, that all the unlabeled bottles had shifted just a tad. I looked for a pattern of movement, attempting to recreate the path of each bottle in order to resolve the sequence of samples, but it was hopeless. I had to toss the whole experiment. I never again failed, throughout my career, to label every sample of every experiment. Science had its poetic aspects, but it also required meticulous discipline. There were no shortcuts.

These were remarkable moments, initiating my life as a scientist. I had a deep sense of belonging in that remote marine laboratory, on a small island in a foreign country, engaged with barnacle metabolism, an esoteric subject to some, but to me a subject that did not need justification. Barnes included me as an author in the article that resulted from our experiments – my first publication – signaling my entrance into the professional world of science. *(10)*

I learned another lesson of a very different sort that summer as well. Our findings showed that barnacles could withstand an oxygen debt far greater than they needed in their natural environment. I extrapolated that in order to be successful, which in barnacle language meant to survive hundreds of millions of years, it was necessary have a greater depth of resources than needed at the moment. If the barnacles were cruising along on minimal supplies for surviving the normal conditions of their environment, they would perish – become extinct – if there were suddenly a significant change, or even a transient change, in environmental conditions. They wouldn't have survived the eons they did on a shoestring budget of resources. Barnacles operated on a surplus. I generalized that success in anything – evolution, competition, career, sports – required a deep reserve, extra resources under the visible surface, a buried foundation to call upon for ultimate success. Nature was no different from life: what you see on the surface isn't enough in the long run.

To appreciate my satisfaction at Millport requires a few words about the preceding month, when I was at Eze-sur-Mer in the south of France near Monte Carlo visiting my mother's family. Uncle Guy had rented a villa that overlooked the Mediterranean, a visual paradise. The house brimmed over with family and friends the month I was there: Guy and his wife Marie-Hélène, Guy's sons David and Édouard, Marie-Hélène's son Philip from a former marriage, a distant cousin, Eli and his mistress, and a small group of guests, including the future Prime Minister of France, Georges Pompidou, who at the time was a close associate of Guy at the bank. A few other guests flowed in and out like the tide. Although the month was meant to be an informal beach vacation, the situation was hardly informal. After my first luncheon outside in the balmy weather I was told politely by Marie-Hélène that I needed to wear a foulard (a neck scarf) and a long-sleeved shirt for meals, even for luncheons on the patio. After each meal, Marie-Hélène discussed the preparation and presentation of the food with the family chef. Political issues were among the more interesting topics of conversation as we ate, but I struggled to comprehend all the French idioms that were rapidly flung around. Mealtime banter also included gossip and various forms of character assassinations. I remember a catty discussion about who had the most and who had the least sexy skin in Parisian society. I won't disclose the winners and losers. Occasionally we went to elegant restaurants in the evenings. My cousin David liked to gamble at Monte Carlo, but I wasn't excited about the possibility of winning (or losing) by chance. I must have been dull company.

In the midst of my stay I came down with typhoid or a related illness, which a local doctor thought I might have contracted from mussels I had eaten at a local restaurant. Confined to bed, I read a layman's book about Einstein and relativity, which kept me sane. Even then, science stood out for me. Marie-Hélène wandered into my room from time to time, curious as to what strange things occupied my mind. I don't think I sold her on physics. Since the consensus was that I shouldn't go to my job with Barnes in Millport until I was cured, I returned to Paris with Guy and Marie-Hélène to recover. My fever receded after a few days in Paris. Although still weak, I decided to go to Scotland. I couldn't miss my golden opportunity for a job in science.

As I stood on deck during the short ferry ride from Wemyss Bay, Scotland, to Millport, the cool breeze blew away any illness that still lingered in me. Being out of touch for those few hours with everyone (cell phones didn't exist yet) gave me a blended sense of freedom and purpose that I've felt only a few times since.

I remember being completely happy. I was on my way to a career in science that I respected and loved. The contrast between the luxurious lifestyle with my Rothschild relatives and my research adventure at Millport made the latter seem as genuine as the former contrived. What I hadn't fully appreciated at the time was how much my Millport experience was an extension of my childhood experiences connected with the sea.

For example, as a very young boy, I loved vacations at coastal Rockport, Maine, in particular catching a small fish on our rowboat and then dissecting my prize. Some afternoons on clear days, Mama tied the rowboat with a short rope to a rock or the wharf and allowed me to go on board and pretend to be rowing on the open ocean having imaginary adventures on the seven seas.

And then in Los Angeles, when I was about twelve or thirteen, Papa and I went fishing for a few days off Catalina Island. That was one of our very few father/son trips, though occasionally we went fishing together for the day on a public boat at the Santa Monica Pier. We rented an outboard motor boat and stayed close to shore: two rubes piloting a boat, knowing nothing about the ocean or boats, anticipating success as novice fishermen. The wind picked up strength as the afternoon progressed, and the ocean became choppy with whitecaps and swells. The boat rocked furiously and I was getting light-headed. We decided to head back. As I reeled in my fishing line, it felt unexpectedly taut. The faster I reeled, the more the fishing pole bent in resistance. Had I caught a big fish? At that moment, a fishing pole attached to my hook jutted from the surface of the water. Not a fish. I had snagged a fiberglass fishing pole, reel and all, from the bottom of the ocean that someone had lost!

We motored back to the dock with our "catch" of the day and took a cab to the hotel. It was then that the full impact of the rocking boat reached home, and I couldn't control my nausea. Suddenly, I vomited – erupted – all over the back seat of the cab. Oh, my god: the smell, the mess! Disgusting. Papa looked green. The driver looked horrified. We apologized profusely, and I assume Papa paid him handsomely for the ride.

So, my father, the famous musician, could also be just plain Papa who was not a better fisherman than I, and who had to contend, on occasion, with vomit as well as applause.

Papa's fascination with the sea influenced my love of marine biology, circa 1935.

Grandpapa (left) and Babushka (right) flanking my uncle Guy in his military uniform, 1940s.

Serge Koussevitzky, music Director of the Boston Symphony
Orchestra, and I in Tanglewood, Massachusetts, circa 1945.

Tennis played a major role for me throughout my high school days, when I competed in tournaments, was highly ranked among the juniors in Southern California, and traveled with the team to the junior national tournaments.

Piatigorsky, You're a Square

The biggest casualty of my time at Harvard was tennis. Competitive tennis had been a major part of my teenage years. I had trained daily, became a highly ranked junior tennis player in Southern California, competed in local tennis tournaments, and once was on a team of junior players playing in the national championships. However, although I was the number one player of the Harvard freshman tennis team (we were undefeated for the season), I quit the varsity team during my sophomore year to devote my time to science. This may seem like a trivial event in my life, but I didn't take it lightly. Tennis was ingrained into my identity. Also, since I was a strong addition to the varsity tennis team, the coach said that I didn't need to come out for daily practices if I showed up for the interscholastic matches. Flattered, I said okay, but practice was essential for playing well, and I felt uncomfortable with this privilege. Therefore, I practiced instead of having lunch, went to laboratory sessions of my science courses in the afternoons, studied at night, and ended in the infirmary with a respiratory illness. I didn't know whether my illness was due to overexertion or just a bug I caught, but in any event, I thought my schedule too demanding and quit the tennis team – goodbye to my identity as a tennis player – a skill that had distinguished me from my peers.

Bypassing tennis was my first experience of choosing one direction over another, foreshadowing similar challenges in my scientific research. Ideas are plentiful in research, and each choice means sacrificing another possibility, without knowing which choice would be more productive. Selective sacrifices – the alternative possibilities not chosen – are seldom mentioned, despite their historical interest and insight into the person making the choices.

An experience I had on the freshman tennis team reflected a family trait that permeated my years in science. The tennis team held an election to choose a captain, an honor I wanted and felt I deserved. But self-promotion – seeking the spotlight – was discouraged in my family. My uncle Guy described an extreme example of not putting himself first in his memoir, *The Whims of Fortune.(11)* When the Germans torpedoed his boat in the Atlantic during the war midway into his crossing from America to England to join the French resistance, he gave his spot on the lifeboat to a crewmember, and consequently floated in the ocean hanging on to a small raft all night. Thankfully a friendly ship rescued him. Later he said that it would have been "ungentlemanly" to take the place from the crew-member.

Conscious of avoiding self-promotion, I voted for my opponent, Mark Woodbury, for captain of the tennis team, rather than for myself, even though it was a secret ballot! A tie vote led to a runoff between Woodbury and me. Again, I voted for Woodbury, conflicted with wanting to win, but thinking it "ungentlemanly" to vote for myself! I won the runoff vote, but never mentioned my circuitous (and lucky) route to victory. I dodged promoting myself, side-stepping even the appearance of self-promotion, throughout my career, when I often nominated others for recognitions I wanted for myself.

Leigh Hoadley, a professor of embryology in the biology department, had a significant influence on me in college. He did not have a strong reputation as a teacher or scholar and tended to ramble. A short obituary in the *Harvard Crimson* (Nov. 10, 1975) implied that Hoadley's devotion to students and his role as Master of Leverett House "cut in to his scientific work in terms of fulfilling potential." James Watson, a Nobel Laureate with Francis Crick and Maurice Wilkins for determining the helical structure of DNA, disparaged Hoadley in his memoir, *Avoid Boring People,* writing, "…conversation followed the lead of Master Hoadley, incapable of either levity or deep thought."[12] Rather harsh! I took Hoadley's undergraduate course in embryology in my junior year and remember him more kindly.

An important moment for me was when he challenged the class by asking what would happen if an early frog embryo were cut in half.

"It would die," I said, which seemed logical (and still does today).

"Not necessarily," said Hoadley. "The two parts of the cut embryo can adjust so that each half develops as a normal embryo, resulting in twins."

"How does that happen?" I asked, suddenly feeling as if I was having a private conversation with the professor.

"I don't know," Hoadley confessed. Then he mentioned "morphochoresis," a term he coined to mean the dance of developing form. The term had an artistic ring, which I liked, although it explained nothing. I never heard anyone else use that expression. Hoadley went on to say that developing twins by splitting an amphibian embryo in half depended on the cleavage plane, and then he talked about the so-called mosaic-type embryos of other species that behaved differently and weren't capable of surviving the knife. Embryos were resilient, some more than others, and mysterious. Hoadley was right: their development was like a dance. His poetic sense, admission of ignorance and appreciation of mystery made biology exciting by giving science depth and wonder and beauty.

In a blurred kind of way, I could see myself as a biologist, perhaps a dancing biologist, or maybe a spectator biologist at a dance performance. I didn't fit any mold, but that was all right, maybe even preferable. It was like my home, with an artistic component. I wasn't following a template.

After Hoadley's introductory course I wanted to take his advanced course in developmental biology. However, he told me that he wouldn't teach it unless at least eight students enrolled. I fell shy of recruiting eight people, but pleaded with him to give the course anyway. He finally consented. We met informally in his office and discussed diverse topics centered on reviews written in *Analysis of Development*.(13) I loved those discussions, which reminded me of Papa's romantic views of science. I started thinking about science as interplay of imaginative ideas, although I understood that science was based on hypotheses, experiments and interpretations, not poetic viewpoints.

Meeting in the intimacy of Hoadley's office to ponder the mysteries of biology rather than listening to formal lectures had a refreshing impact. The unanswered questions about embryonic development were like a lure to a hungry fish. Instead of a final exam (how I hated those), I wrote a term paper that considered the following: If half an amphibian egg could form a whole embryo, and if some lizards and embryonic frogs could regenerate a tail, why shouldn't a person be able to regenerate an arm or a leg? In today's language, how could one activate the right cascade of genes to grow a new limb from an amputated stump? I predicted that in the future a human amputee would be a transient reminder of the medical dark ages that existed at the time I was taking the course. I was beginning to think about science more practically, even as Hoadley portrayed science for me as beautiful mysteries that could be whittled into ambitious dreams.

My senior year at Harvard was decision time for my future career. A number of classmates applied to medical school, and Hoadley advised me to do the same. He said that being a physician would give me license to practice medicine as well as to mix academic medicine with research, while a PhD degree would limit me to research.

"You never know," he said, "when you might want or need to practice medicine." True, but it didn't inspire me.

I listed the pros and cons for being a physician or a basic scientist. I imagined that if I were a physician peering into a microscope I might ask myself, "What's wrong – sick

– with those cells?" If I were a PhD staring at the same sample I might wonder, "What's right – *healthy* – with those cells?" Perhaps these questions were just two sides of the same coin and posing the question the way I did mere sophistry. Certainly, physicians have made basic discoveries, and basic scientists have made medical advances. Yet, I needed to choose between these two alternative career pathways – MD or PhD. I preferred the idea of spending my life immersed in health rather than disease, although I didn't realize at the time how different these two alternative careers actually were.

I decided to apply to graduate school for a PhD rather than medical school.

I set my sights on the California Institute of Technology (Caltech), well aware of the stiff competition for admission. Apart from being a scientific powerhouse, Caltech would force me to confront my difficulties in the physical sciences and math. It wasn't that I envisioned approaching research in terms of physics or math – I never would have succeeded by doing that – but I didn't want to become a biologist by default, in other words, because the physical sciences were too difficult for me. A Caltech degree would satisfy me that I hadn't shirked the aspects of science I found most difficult. The major attraction for me at Caltech was developmental biology, not the physical sciences, and a Caltech professor, Albert Tyler, who was well known for his research on fertilization, especially of sea urchin eggs. He was a tempting potential mentor for me, due to my interest in development and marine biology. Not very professionally, I dropped in on Tyler without an appointment when I was in Los Angeles visiting my parents. He had no idea who I was. By chance, I found him in his office.

"Excuse me," I said, "I'm a senior at Harvard and was in the neighborhood and would like to get my PhD at Caltech working with you."

What chutzpah! He looked surprised, rolled his bulging eyes and wrinkled his brow. Despite my intrusion, he was gracious and unpretentious, and it seemed to me, even a little self-conscious. He's a kind man, I thought, with a quirky manner, suggesting that, like Hoadley, he was not a popular mentor. He didn't have the "slick" style that I associate with those who feel they're riding the crest. Tyler told me about sea urchins and fertilization and gave me an impressive handful of reprints of his published articles. I felt excited, yet overwhelmed. He had written more than I'd read. The mountain looked impossibly high from where I stood, not unlike the challenge to meet the high bar of my family's accomplishments.

I asked Tyler if he had space for another student.

"I can't accept a graduate student on my own," he said. "You have to apply to Caltech through the regular channels."

I knew that, but liked the idea of bypassing formality!

Tyler introduced me to Ray Owen, the chairman of the Biology Department, who also was willing to talk to me then without an appointment. I asked him, "Would I have to take the graduate record examinations (GREs) if I applied to Caltech?"

This was my first encounter with graduate schools and I

had not done my homework. Everyone took GREs for application to graduate school.

"Not take the GREs?" Owen looked confused.

"Yes," I pursued.

"No one has ever asked me that before," he said.

I had never considered that before. It was an impulsive thought, based on the fear I would never be accepted to Caltech due to my poor performances on standardized tests. Maybe if I could find a way to never take them...so I persisted.

"But would you still consider my application if I didn't take the GREs?"

My reasoning was to let the admissions board assume that my GRE results would be commensurate with my academic record at Harvard (*cum laude* in biology, despite the dismal prediction of the aptitude tests I took as a freshman), rather than receive poor GRE results, an unfortunate possibility that plagued me with all the standardized tests I'd ever taken.

"There's no written requirement to take them that I know of," Owen said, scratching his head. "But every applicant does."

In parting, I asked him about my chances for acceptance in general.

"Well, we turned down Jim Watson."

Ouch!

When my peers went to take the GREs, I escaped to the Brattle theater next to Harvard Square to catch a Humphrey Bogart movie.

What was I thinking? It's still hard for me to believe that I was so cavalier about what meant so much to me.

Perhaps this was an unconscious example of taking an alternate route, not following the established protocol – a silent rebellion that resembled in some way Papa's path to success.

Despite the absurd risk-taking, I was admitted to Caltech. My guess is that Hoadley gave me a strong recommendation and that Tyler supported me within the admission committee. I'll assume my unconventional "drop-in" paid off and be eternally grateful. Caltech graduate students were all accepted on full scholarships, and also received small stipends for being a teaching assistant. It was the first time that I felt equal with my peers and worthy in my own right, which meant so much more to me than the money.

Tyler arranged for me to spend the summer at the Woods Hole Biological Laboratories on Cape Cod, a vibrant scientific center, before starting my graduate work at Caltech. He enrolled me in the "Fertilization and Gamete Physiology Training Program" organized by his former PhD student, Charles Metz, a professor at the University of Miami. It was apparent that science operated by selective networks, and I was fortunate to be incorporated into Tyler's. My mentor in the research-training program was C.R. Austin (nicknamed "Bunny"), who was the Charles Darwin Professor at Oxford University and an authority on mammalian fertilization.

Austin suggested that I try to identify the cause of a rapid, physical modification in sea urchin spermatozoa at the beginning of the fertilization process. When contacting the jelly coat (called fertilizin) on the surface of the egg, the spermatozoan shoots-out a narrow tube from its tip – a "jack -in-box" spring-like shape change. The tip of the tube then fuses with the surface membrane of the egg, making the spermatozoon and egg one cell even before the internal contents of the spermatozoon (essentially the DNA) has entered the egg.

I discovered that summer that dissolved fertilizin triggered the reaction, which raised numerous questions. What caused the shape change? Did the fertilizin bind to a specific receptor on the surface of the sperm, as Tyler thought – an anti-fertilizin? Could other proteins elicit this reaction as well? Could spermatozoa that had already undergone the shape change acrosome reaction still fertilize the egg? My two-dimensional view of a research problem became much more complex and harbored numerous nested questions, much as a series of Russian dolls, one inside the other. This summer of research changed my naïve notion that fertilization was a straightforward event to the realistic understanding that it is a complex process that required a lifetime of study.

My discovery may not have been revolutionary, but it was a step forward in knowledge. I had discovered something no one in the world knew before, a singular achievement: dissolved fertilizin initiated the reaction causing a shape change in sea urchin sperm. For me, fertilizin had become like dust on the moon's surface for Neil Armstrong. So that was what science was all about! Being an explorer. Discovery. Personal achievement.

The students in the research course at Woods Hole presented their findings to the scientific community at the end of the summer. I split my research results into two fifteen-minute talks that were published in separate abstracts in the Woods Hole journal, *Biological Bulletin*. I had a small audience, as expected for student presentations, and my first talk went well enough. I saw some nods in the audience, and I received a question or two. My second talk followed the first. Maybe I was less enthusiastic, or maybe the findings were less interesting, but after a couple of minutes I noticed a gentleman in the back row had closed his eyes. Was he bored? I couldn't tolerate that. What to do? I gave a summary last sentence in midstream and sat down. My fifteen-minute presentation lasted about three minutes.

"What happened?" asked my perplexed mentor and co-author, C. R. Austin. "Why didn't you go through with the talk?"

"The guy in the back looked like he was going to sleep," I said, feeling embarrassed.

"That's ridiculous. There will always be some scientists who are not interested in your particular work, or just have something else on their mind at the moment."

That made sense. What I didn't tell Austin, and didn't realize myself at the time, was that Papa's image haunted me. His concerts and eloquent storytelling led to standing ovations and captivated audiences. I didn't want to be boring. An aversion to boring anyone persisted my entire career and contributed to stage fright before any presentation I gave, no matter the audience. However, I took this stage fright as incentive to prepare thoroughly for every talk I gave, often too thoroughly, resulting in presenting too much information and thus speaking too quickly. It took me years to gain enough confidence to slow down and limit my focus.

There were a few instances throughout my career when someone from the audience told me after a lecture, "You should be proud. I've heard your father play many times and you are as accomplished in your field as he was in his."

That meant a lot to me, but believing it was another matter. Also, as satisfying as it was to hear this, especially from a stranger, it told me that I was not alone in comparing myself with Papa. The pride of being his son was inseparable with the challenge of being his equal, both in my mind and in the mind of others.

While I loved immersion in research at Woods Hole, small human exchanges – "little things" – were important. Once on a sunny day, I sneaked away from my peers in the training program and went for a swim at the beach. I waded into the cool salt water, my body warmed by the sun, feeling at peace with the world. Suddenly, I heard the voice of Alberto Monroy, an instructor in the training program and professor at the University of Palermo.

"Skipping work, eh?" he said, knee-deep in the water behind me.

"What? Just for a quick swim. It's so beautiful out here," I stammered, embarrassed to be caught playing hooky.

"Your experiments in good shape?" he asked.

"I know I'm supposed to be in the lab," I said, falling short of answering his question.

"Only technicians would stay in the lab on a day like today," he said. "The real scientists would be out here!"

Such an innocuous statement, more social than meaningful, and yet...

Why would I remember that small episode so many years later? Perhaps for the same reason that informal discussions in Hoadley's office humanized dispassionate science for me, or perhaps being considered a real scientist by an accomplished scientist like Monroy, or perhaps I valued kindness over judgment.

Although for different reasons, I believe that Albert Tyler, like me, felt the pressure of high expectations. He was a graduate student of the legendary geneticist, Thomas Hunt Morgan, who moved from Columbia University with Tyler to establish the Caltech Biology Department in 1928. Tyler received his PhD in 1929, the first doctorate degree given by the new Department of Biology under Morgan. Morgan received the 1933 Nobel Prize in Medicine or Physiology for his contributions to the role of chromosomes in heredity. Tyler remained at Caltech his entire career in the long shadow of Morgan, which probably dangled a frustratingly high scientific goal for him.

Since Tyler was my PhD mentor, Morgan was my scientific grandfather – another celebrity, albeit more distant, connected with my life.

On rare occasions Tyler exposed vulnerable feelings. One anecdote is telling. Tyler and I were discussing his efforts to engineer sea urchin eggs by soaking them in seawater with genetic messages (messenger RNAs). Tyler was experimenting with an early form of "euphenics," as he called it, namely trying to make the embryos synthesize artificial proteins by engineering beyond the level of the gene. The more commonly known "eugenics" tampers with the genes *per se* – genetic engineering – a lively field today. Tyler's experiments were visionary but subject to alternative interpretations. Although aware of this, he procrastinated performing critical control experiments to establish that his interpretations were correct.

I didn't let it go.

"Why not just do the control experiments and settle the issue? You don't know what will work and what won't," I insisted, most likely overstepping my bounds as a graduate student.

"Well, it's complicated," he said, without much conviction.

"How is it complicated?"

He paused. "I guess I'm scared of the results."

Tyler's surprising admission warned me to not confuse my ego with my hypotheses or ideas or ambition. Tyler raised the red flag that science is mired with risk and emotions. Yet, it is that passion for science and pride mixed with ambition that drives the investigator for years on end, often obsessively, to tease the truth from nature and develop a personal identity in the work.

For my PhD dissertation, I investigated fertilization of sea urchin eggs, Tyler's specialty. Under natural conditions, the spermatozoon triggers events in the egg that activates protein synthesis. How did the fertilized egg do this?

Tyler's laboratory had shown that the sudden burst of protein synthesis after fertilization did not require a corresponding burst of gene activity to make new messenger RNA – the templates directing protein synthesis. New synthesis of protein without new messenger RNA was unique and must have meant that inactive messenger RNA was already present in the unfertilized egg. My project was to discover how that inactive messenger was activated at fertilization.

Unexpected twists in my experiments led to a new finding unrelated to protein synthesis: fertilization released a barrier for the uptake of nucleosides (the building blocks for DNA and RNA) by the egg. Tyler arranged that I go to the Friday Harbor Laboratories at Puget Sound off the coast of Washington to work with his colleague and former postdoctoral fellow, Arthur Whiteley, a professor at the University of Washington. He was an expert on membrane transport in sea urchin eggs, the issue I was dealing with. I welcomed a break from the smog at Pasadena and was anxious to go once again to a marine lab.

I loved the marine environment and total immersion in science at Friday Harbor, as I did in Millport when I was an undergraduate. The humid, salty air, the calm water of Puget Sound, the brilliant colors of the diverse marine organisms in the holding tanks used for the students and researchers, and the boat excursions with the scientists and students collecting invertebrates – a secluded haven. Working day and night, I discovered that nucleoside uptake by the sea urchin egg at fertilization depended on a phosphorylation reaction. I published my findings with Whiteley, which became a chapter of my PhD thesis.*(14)*

One evening I felt the force of nature as never before. With a quiet sunset in progress, I hopped into a rowboat with a fishing pole to relax and enjoy the evening. Drifting not far from shore, my fishing line out with a baited hook, I heard a mysterious whoosh. A minute later, the sound returned slightly louder. I was trying to identify the source, when the head of a whale rose from the water's surface a few yards from me. As I stared in awe at the black head, I heard another *whoosh* – much louder, and clearly coming from the whale's blowhole spraying water droplets. I felt like an ant about to be crushed by a giant. My fishing line was under the whale. What if he (she?) wants a snack and takes the bait? I reeled in my fishing line *very* slowly not to attract the whale's attention. I didn't want the whale to play a game called "knock the boat in the air with my tail." I rowed as gently as I could (how naïve) as I headed back towards the dock. Much to my chagrin, a number of people on shore saw the incident and found it funny: the whale was well known in the area and considered harmless, like a local pet. Some pet! I never forgot the sheer power and strength of the beast that roamed beneath me, and the humble feeling of being such a minuscule part of nature.

One of the best evenings of my fifty-years in science occurred when I had dinner alone in the laboratory after a long day of experiments. I went to greet the students and scientists returning from a day's collecting in Puget Sound on the research boat, curious as always what marine specimens they came back with. They had amassed many large shrimps, so the captain gave me a bowl full of the squirming critters. Back in the lab I cooked them in seawater heated over a Bunsen burner, Mozart's Don Giovanni playing on the radio. I never had a more satisfying meal or felt more content than immersed in music and eating fresh shrimp in that marine laboratory. I couldn't imagine a career more suited to me than being a scientist by the side of the sea, searching for answers to questions about nature's ways, and discovering new questions that few even knew existed.

I co-authored five articles with Tyler as a graduate student and one after receiving my PhD. I sat by Tyler's side in his office co-writing our articles, discussing every sentence. I am very grateful to him for such a privileged tutorial. It was an extraordinary education on writing a scientific article, which I reciprocated later by devoting quality time to my own students and postdoctoral fellows writing their articles.

Despite my good relationship with Tyler, a difficult situation arose once, which concerned a theory I called "the revolving door hypothesis." It was known that acidic, neutral and basic amino acids, the building blocks of proteins, were transported into cells through separate surface membrane channels. I proposed that each of these channels was separate, undefined "revolving doors," and that when one "door" started "revolving" it would spit out amino acids of the same kind inside the egg. Tyler liked the idea, since he agreed to have his technician perform experiments to test the hypothesis over a couple of weeks when he went out of town. I was busy with other experiments and happy to have the help. The experiments worked as I had hoped – transport of amino acids in the sea water into the egg was associated with extrusion of amino acids of the same type (acidic, basic or neutral) from the egg – although we had no idea what mechanism was in play. We decided to publish an article proposing the conceptual hypothesis. The trouble started when we finished writing the manuscript.

"Who will be the first author?" Tyler asked, after he placed the final period on the page.

I was taken aback. It was my idea and he had agreed to let his technician do the experiments to save time while he was traveling. How should I react? I was afraid to be too assertive, and thinking, "Are you kidding? I should be first author."

But instead, I said, "I don't know. What do you think?"

"Well, my technician did all the experiments," he said.

I was tongue-tied, my heart racing. "It's my baby!" I screamed silently. If Tyler placed himself first it would appear as if he generously tacked me on to help his student.

"Let's flip a coin," he said.

Flip a coin! What if I lost?

"Okay," I said, suppressing my growing rage.

He removed a coin from his pocket. "Heads or tails?"

"Heads," I said.

He caught the coin on its descent and flipped it onto his extended arm. "Heads," he announced.

I was first author. *(15)*

I'll never know whether Tyler would have put his name first if he'd won the coin toss. In fact, as I recall the event, I never saw the coin after he flipped it. Perhaps it was tails, but he called heads. Why do we always assume we know so much? I have often thought back on this episode to remind me, once again, not to let ambition cloud my science or professional decisions, and not to play games with authorship. The issue is too sensitive. Thus, I learned as a graduate student that science is not a selfless, dispassionate rendezvous with nature. Tyler showed me unwittingly that science is subject to the pitfalls of ambition with all its triumphs and disappointments, like any other profession.

Tyler had a kind side. One Saturday he and I went to collect a peculiar, cigar-shaped worm (*Urechis caupo*) that builds a U-shaped tunnel as its home in the intertidal zone of muddy beaches. While we were driving to the mudflats, our conversation drifted to what makes a successful scientist. At first Tyler said that mathematical skills were critical, but then, as if sensing my discomfort of being a non-mathematical type, he quickly changed his tune.

"No," he said. "The successful scientist is the one who has the patience to work steadily to complete the often-boring work that is needed."

I had recently spent many hours determining optical densities for innumerable samples in my research (similar to what I did in Millport studying barnacles). What I heard Tyler say, then, was that he believed in me. Being a graduate student with a package of insecurities common to students (and often mature scientists as well), I appreciated this encouragement, which was on a par with Alberto Monroy telling me that a "real scientist" would be out for a swim on a sunny day at the beach rather than slaving in the lab.

It's curious that I remember trivial experiences as important life events when they touched my vulnerabilities.

A few other memories from Caltech etched in my mind. One involves my role as a graduate teaching assistant in an undergraduate laboratory course in physiology. The professor instructed me to give each student two grades: one for the laboratory notebook, and the other an appraisal of their work in the laboratory. I had no trouble giving an objective laboratory notebook grade; the appraisal grade was another matter. Caltech undergraduates are renowned for being bright, promising scientists. How to assess these stellar students?

"I see, Joram, that you gave each student an A for his work in the laboratory," said the professor at the completion of the course.

"Yes."

"Do you want to rethink that?" he continued.

"No," I said, starting to feel uncomfortable.

"Are they all so good?"

"As far as I could tell, they all did excellent work in the laboratory," I said. "I can't say one is better than the other."

"But still, *everyone* an A?"

I didn't know how to appease the professor. I knew that my overly generous stream of A's was unorthodox, but I also had no idea which student deserved a higher or lower subjective grade for work in the laboratory.

And then I recalled the despair of a music student who had received a B in Papa's cello master class at the University of Southern California. The despondent student told Papa that he needed an A to keep his scholarship.

"I gave you a B?" Papa asked the student.

"Yes."

"Let me see the report card."

He scratched over the B with a pen to make it an A. "It must have been an error," he said, and handed the report card back to the student.

Problem solved. Papa was probably hardly aware of the difference between an A and B, and if he was, I doubt he cared. Cellists were people – artists – not letters, not grades. I don't know if the student went on to a successful career in music.

The professor waited for my decision on what grade I would give each student for his work in the lab.

"Well," I stalled, "some – most – deserve an A, and I suppose the others need it." More chutzpah! I was not going to change my appraisals, and in any case, I didn't know who should get what grade.

"Okay," said the professor, looking annoyed.

I was not asked to be a teaching assistant in that course the following year.

The final hurdle to obtain my PhD was the customary oral examination covering my thesis. *(16)*

The examiners included Albert Tyler, James Bonner, Norman Horowitz (who had been Tyler's graduate student years earlier), Sterling Emerson and Henry Borsook, all eminent scientists. Confident but nervous, I came to the examination dressed in a coat and tie. When I walked into the conference room, James Bonner took one look at me and said, "Piatigorsky, you're a square; you always were a square and will always be a square."

I think it's self-evident what Bonner meant by "a square." It wasn't a compliment.

In an interminable moment between being ridiculed by Bonner and queried by the Caltech professors, I remembered a picture in the yearbook from the first grade at Friends Select School. I was in a coat and tie and short pants at the tip-top of a Jungle Jim. My classmates were in T-shirts and jeans. Raised formally as a French child in informal America, I dressed like a "Bonner square" already in the first grade!

And then Papa flashed through my mind. When I had accompanied him at the Casals Music Festival a few months earlier, he rehearsed in the heat of Puerto Rico in a coat and tie when others were in short-sleeve shirts.

"I never perform informally, no matter how hot it is," he said. "Rehearsal is preparation for what's to come. I don't know what the conditions will be, so I might as well be prepared."

If Papa didn't compromise his professional self-discipline, why should I? The PhD oral examination was my performance at that moment, as well as a rehearsal for the future. A coat and tie were appropriate and respectful to the audience, and I adhered to that discipline throughout my career.

Norman Horowitz asked the last question of my oral exam: "Do you think there's life on other planets?" He was one of the scientists seeking extraterrestrial life at the time and was pessimistic that it existed.

"It's possible," I said.

"Really?" he responded, perking up.

I had recently read a speculation that the high reactivity and atomic structure of silicon that might, under proper conditions, substitute for carbon, which is essential for life on Earth.

"What if there was life based on silicon instead of carbon?" I ventured.

He remained silent.

"It might work in reverse to life as we know it," I said, starting to feel excited about giving my imagination free reign.

He looked curious.

"Well, life on Earth," I continued, "is based on the low reactivity of carbon and by having enzymes catalyze – speed up – biochemical reactions when they are needed. But what if silicon was used as the backbone for life on another planet rather than carbon, as its atomic structure suggests might be possible? Since silicon is so reactive, relative to carbon, a silicon-structured life would depend on suppressing reactions – slowing them down or inhibiting them altogether. When a particular biochemical reaction was needed, the suppressor of that reaction would 'lift its lid,' so to speak, which would allow the reaction to occur."

It sounded pretty ingenious to me! Life based on relieving suppressors.

Horowitz didn't holler with delight. "Wouldn't work," he said. "It's not thermodynamically stable."

And that ended my student days. I was now Dr. Piatigorsky, in a coat and tie, but apparently still in need of some training in thermodynamics.

One last point: Papa knew nothing of science, but in my opinion, he deserved the dedication I gave him at the front of my thesis: "To Father." This came as a surprise to Papa when he opened the bound thesis I gave him. For me, it overpowered the many times we failed to communicate, and represented, perhaps too formally, my love and gratitude for his question: "What about the speed of dark?"

Tyler congratulated me at the Caltech commencement, having no inkling that I would be his last PhD to graduate, as well as a mentor to his last unfinished PhD student. When I had my diploma in hand, Tyler said, "Great accomplishment, Joram, but you know that degrees are only useful to those who will never work again." I was struck by how much his cryptic comment resembled my father's tongue-in-cheek remark on how academic credentials diminish stature. Also, it brought to mind a comment Hoadley made in response to a letter I had sent him about my initial research at Caltech.

Hoadley wrote, "I am delighted to read that you are 'having fun' for all of this investigation is fun; just remember that you must never be entirely convinced of the truth of your own conclusions but just keep on trying to make the picture more complete. The picture will still be incomplete when you too, retire from the scene! At least one can hope that it will be." At the conclusion of his letter, he wrote, "Well, here's to you Joram. And continue to have a grand time with your investigations. Please, no BREAK-THROUGHS, and please don't become a 'researcher'. I have great difficulty taking either one of those terms! Good luck and do write me again someday when the spirit moves. I promise to reply."

Good old Hoadley: like Papa, like Tyler. Work hard and keep perspective, they said. Credentials don't make the man. Stay humble. Perhaps trite, but important advice.

I never forgot my mentors' words throughout my journey as a scientist. From these important people in my life I also drew a lesson of my own.

Don't minimize kindness as a critical ingredient in whatever I undertake.

My Ph.D. mentor Albert Tyler at my Caltech graduation, 1967.

Love at First Sight

After having spent a summer at the Friday Harbor Laboratories, the University of Washington tempted me with an informal offer, via Tyler, of an assistant professorship once I had a PhD, bypassing the customary postdoctoral work. Although flattered, I had set my sights on expanding my research experience as a postdoctoral fellow rather than seeking an immediate faculty position in academia. Tyler suggested I apply for a postdoctoral position at the National Institutes of Health (NIH). "It's a world-class research center, Joram, where you could devote all your time to research and expand your scientific horizons. Also, you might be able to get in on the ground floor of a new Institute," he said. Tyler had been a consultant for establishing the National Institute of Child Health and Human Development, which was created as a consequence of President Kennedy's baby boy, Patrick, dying of hyaline membrane disease the day after his birth. In addition to NIH being a strong scientific institution, the possibility existed that I could join the Public Health Service (PHS), obviating the threat of being drafted for the Vietnam War that was raging at the time.

I also had a scientific reason for targeting NIH for postdoctoral work. Alfred Coulombre (known as "Chris"), renowned for his studies on eye development in chickens at NIH, provided an opportunity to extend my graduate research on fertilization to development of lens cells later in development. Tyler thought that experimenting on differentiating lens cells might be a good way to test his hypothesis that embryonic cells activated suppressed – "masked" – messenger RNAs during their differentiation, as sea urchin eggs activated "masked" messenger RNA after fertilization. The key to the proposed project was that large amounts of easily recognized proteins, called crystallins, accumulated in the lens cells to confer their optical properties. (Crystallins derived their name from their abundance in the crystal-clear lens. Science isn't always technical!). Showing that lens differentiation involved activating "masked" messenger RNAs would represent significant progress in understanding cellular differentiation and connect processes that occurred at fertilization with those taking place during later development.

Although the project seemed promising in theory, Coulombre was a histologist, not a molecular biologist, and used microscopic analyses of fixed tissues as endpoints for virtually all his experiments. The techniques for the molecular studies I planned were not going on in his laboratory. "Learn the biology from Coulombre," Tyler had said, "and be prepared to learn new experimental techniques for the rest of your life in science." It was true that eye biology would not change, while techniques are constantly improving, so I figured that I might as well get used to being challenged early on with learning new methods any way I could. Molecular cloning and the onslaught of the computer age turned out to be dramatic examples proving Tyler's point. Technology whizzes ahead.

Coulombre accepted me as a postdoctoral fellow, and I became one of few PhDs in the PHS program at NIH (the government loves using initials!). Since the PHS was designed to expose MDs to research, a physician received one-third more salary than a PhD to compensate for foregoing the more lucrative practice of medicine. In 1967, then, I became a postdoctoral fellow at NIH, valued at two-thirds of my physician peers.

I'd hoped to take advantage of a technically complex experimental system established in Coulombre's laboratory in which lens cells removed from chicken embryos continued to develop and mature in culture. After removing the eye lens from the embryo, it had to be dissected into its two parts: a thin, one-cell layer of cuboidal epithelial cells (called the lens epithelia) in the front of the lens, and a thick layer of elongated cells (called the lens fiber cells) behind. This delicate process was a difficult procedure that involved subtle eye-hand coordination that had to be performed with sharpened jeweler's forceps under a dissecting microscope. Once the fragile lens epithelia, which was easily damaged during dissection, was obtained, it was tacked down in a plastic dish, another delicate process, and cultured in growth medium. The lens epithelial cells elongated in culture, mimicking their normal differentiation into lens fiber cells. It was likely (although not confirmed) that the cultured cells also had a burst of crystallin synthesis, as occurred in the normal process of lens cell differentiation.

I wanted to determine whether "masked" (inactive) messenger RNAs directing crystallin synthesis were present in the cuboidal epithelial cells and became activated when the cells elongated into lens fiber cells.

When Coulombre first introduced me to this experimental system, he patiently showed me how to remove the lens from a chicken embryo, and then asked me to remove the lens from the other eye.

"No problem," I said.

I peered into the dissecting microscope and started manipulating the forceps, but I was clumsy at first and I pierced the eye in several places. The hardest part was coordinating slight hand movements. After some fumbling, I managed to remove the lens and place it in the plastic dish filled with clear saline solution.

Elated, I started looking for the isolated lens in the dish to admire my newly acquired skill but couldn't find it. I moved the dish around under the microscope searching, baffled.

"It's gone!" I exclaimed to Coulombre.

He just smiled.

"I'm not kidding. I can't find it anywhere in the dish. I know I put it here, but..."

Suddenly I saw a magnified piece of dust under the clear dish.

"Of course!" I blurted out.

I realized at that moment that I couldn't see the lens because it was transparent, virtually invisible. But the invisible lens was also a tiny magnifying glass, so the dust under it was enlarged. How amazing was that! The transparent lens made up of an encapsulated mass of cells was comparable to a magnifying glass. How ingenious to have evolved such an eye structure to focus images on the retina. But that was not what really captivated me: I fell in love with the invisible lens at first sight.

I worked for months to master the technology. The long days into the night staring into the microscope were physically grueling, although satisfying in that I had time to roam from one subject to another in my mind. The problem was that the experimental system was geared for small sample sizes used for histology, not for the large amounts of tissue I needed to study gene expression. There was no precedence then that such minuscule amounts of material could be used for the molecular studies I wanted to do. DNA cloning technology had not been invented yet. Thus, the odds were stacked against me – ironically, the tiny epithelia comprised a meal too large for my plate. Yet, I was proud of my new expertise at microsurgery, a skill that became important many years later when I investigated scallop and jellyfish eyes.

Despite the difficulty of the project, Coulombre gave me my first opportunity to make all the decisions for my research, an invaluable experience in distinguishing what's interesting from what's possible at the time – to blend pipedreams with reality. I had a lot to learn. Progress crawled and often led to insufficient and contradictory data as I struggled to obtain enough lens explants for my experiments. I was in a quandary. Should I continue my efforts, or should I abandon my research project? If I decided to start a new project, what would it be? I was still under Tyler's influence and had not yet found my own direction. What seemed promising at first now looked confusing.

Nonetheless, my mind clung to sticking with the lens. It had many advantages for studying development, notably elongation of the cells and strong expression of a few genes encoding the crystallins. These traits were easy to measure and provided a handle to study the mechanics of lens development. What I needed to do was step back and look at research with fresh eyes.

**Mama's smile reveals her pride on my receiving a Ph.D.
from Caltech, 1967.**

No Time to Rush

As I pondered new directions for my research, Papa asked me whether I knew personally the other scientists involved with my doctorate.

"I know quite a few of them in the United States," I said, "but not the Europeans."

Papa's question was consistent with the many times he suggested that I branch out and not become "one track minded," as he called my tendency to focus intensely on one interest at a time, whether it was flying model airplanes as a young boy or learning exclusively from one tennis professional during my competitive tournament-tennis days as a teenager or being blinded by "masked" messenger RNA. By contrast, Papa's unique, precarious early life influenced his broad outlook and pragmatism. He performed internationally as a "citizen of the world" with his Nansen Passport, which gave him an identity without borders. Branching out was Papa's lifestyle and mode of survival.

I sensed the advantages of seeing beyond what was directly in front of me. Also, I welcomed the idea of a short break from the difficulty of my research project. I wrote to a few of the European scientists whose work I had relied on for my thesis research, and they promptly replied that they would welcome my visit. Tore Hultin, John Runnström, and Bjorn Afselius were in Stockholm. Giovanni Giudice, a professor at the University of Palermo in Sicily, asked me to give a lecture on my research. Naturally, I accepted.

My first stop was to meet Giudice, an energetic and charismatic scientist. In the taxi from the airport to the university, the cab driver wove in and out of traffic like a madman, and I prayed for a safe arrival. Suddenly, he clipped a man on a bicycle, not hard, but just enough to knock him down. Did the driver stop? No!

"Stupido!" He yelled and kept going. Then he had another "minor" collision – this time with a horse. Apparently, there was no harm done, and the driver sped on.

Palermo needed speed bumps on their streets!

Giudice couldn't have been nicer. We talked about science, about Palermo, and about the Zoological Station in Naples, a marine laboratory established in 1872 that I wanted to visit but never did. It was a wonderful experience to feel like a colleague instead of a student, and to hear that my work had some presence in the world of science. I never believed individuals who seemed oblivious to recognition, and I never claimed to be one. I believe that exposure – putting oneself on the line, so to speak – is important, if not necessary, to reach higher levels of accomplishment, and then to have some recognition for one's effort.

"Okay," said Giudice. "Time for your lecture. Do you speak Italian?"

"Oops, no. Not a word. I do speak some French," I said. "Would that help?"

"Ah, yes. Perfect. Please, give your lecture in French."

This was the first and only lecture I ever gave in French. From the questions received, I think it seemed comprehensible.

In Stockholm, I first met Runnström, the grand old man, a pioneer in development. The desk in his large office was surrounded with shelves filled with reprints of his publications – hundreds and hundreds of articles. He greeted me cordially and said, "But you're so young, and you've done so much already."

Who would have guessed that someone thought that on another continent?

My publications had reached across the Atlantic. I was flattered but didn't feel that I'd done much yet. I felt like a young scientist with wet ink on my diploma, though I was reassured that I had entered the right profession and, again, was in the right place at the right time – in a universe that blended my effort with nature's magic.

What I remember about Afzelius, apart from his excellent electron micrographs, is that he walked so fast through the streets of Stockholm that I struggled to keep a pace. That was my goal scientifically as well: to keep up.

And meeting Hultin put his important articles in context that made him approachable.

Science was my world now and I wouldn't have had it any other way.

I wouldn't have contacted these scientists or gone to Sicily and Stockholm to meet them if Papa hadn't suggested it. I was skeptical at first, but he was right. Being there, knowing the people, bursting the bubble of estrangement, provided a deeper connection with the work. It was like taking a course in the intimacy of Hoadley's office, where we discussed ideas and pondered what we didn't know, rather than meeting in a large lecture hall where facts and figures flashed on the screen as abstractions. "Being there" made science personal – both creative and fallible – rather than a stranger's voice in the murky distance.

Before meeting these scientists, I went to Tel-Aviv to visit my aunt Bethsabée. At that time Tyler and I were finishing a draft of my sixth publication of my PhD research. I had a sense of urgency to finish this article while flying to Israel, worked steadily on it the entire flight and mailed a completed draft to Tyler as soon as the plane landed. Tyler made a few revisions, mailed it back to me, and went to participate in a faculty/student softball game at Caltech (I believe he was the pitcher). He left the game feeling ill and suffered a lethal heart attack when he got home. He was 62. He passed away before I received the modified manuscript in the mail.

I arranged with John Saunders, the Editor-in-Chief of the scientific journal, *Developmental Biology*, to publish a memorial issue in tribute to Tyler, filled with articles his students had been invited to submit.(17) Linus Pauling, Tyler's longtime associate at Caltech, accepted my invitation to write an introduction, an honor that would have pleased Tyler immensely. I co-authored the leadoff article with Tyler in the issue.(18) Thus, I was the last student to receive a PhD from Tyler, capping that lineage of Morgan's scientific grandchildren. I took over Tyler's commitment to write a book chapter on gametogenesis, which I wrote largely in the magnificent Library of Congress in Washington; it became my last scientific work connected with sea urchins. *(19)*

My urgency to send my revised manuscript to Tyler wasn't a new sensation. I often felt rushed to finish any task. While this kept procrastinating at bay, I believe that rushing is an enemy of creativity, which under ideal circumstances has no destination or absolute end point – no deadline. What's the rush? Whatever the creative task, it can always be improved, polished, made more interesting. The Tyler experience made me conscious of my predisposition to rush. To that end, I have kept two "rules" in mind ever since. The first Papa heard from Igor Stravinsky, which I presume he said in jest.

"I have so much to do," said Stravinsky. "I have no time to rush!"

Great truth couched in humor.

The second is Aleksandr Solzhenitsyn's "Rule of the Final Inch" in *The First Circle*, which has guided me for as long as I can remember, and which I gave to my postdoctoral fellows when they thought their manuscripts were completed. I believe this rule is critical for any creative effort and sufficiently important to quote here.

"Now listen to the rule of the last inch. The realm of the last inch. The job is almost finished, the goal almost attained, everything possible seems to have been achieved, every difficulty overcome — and yet the quality is just not there. The work needs more finish, perhaps further research. In that moment of weariness and self-satisfaction, the temptation is greatest to give up, not to strive for the peak of quality. That's the realm of the last inch — here, the work is very, very complex, but it's also particularly valuable because it's done with the most perfect means. The rule of the last inch is simply this — not to leave it undone. And not to put it off — because otherwise your mind loses touch with that realm. And not to mind how much time you spend on it, because the aim is not to finish the job quickly, but to reach perfection." [20]

In my laboratory at the National Institutes of Health, circa 1982.

Any Little Discovery

When I returned to NIH, I was inspired to refocus my research. Marshall Nirenberg, a Nobel Laureate for his discovery of the triplet genetic code, had proposed a novel mechanism using transfer RNAs to control the cellular synthesis of specialized proteins. I thought that Nirenberg's hypothesis might be tested in the chicken lens cells and asked him whether he would be willing to collaborate, a presumptuous request for a rookie postdoctoral fellow to make to a Nobel Prize winner. Nonetheless, Nirenberg listened politely. A paraphrase of our conversation went as follows.

Nirenberg asked, "How much lens tissue can you get?"

"I'm not sure. The embryonic chicken lens and, especially the explants, are very small."

I'd suffered through that problem already!

"Can you get hundreds of milligrams – grams – of tissue per experiment?"

"Oh, no. These lenses and explants are really, really tiny."

I didn't actually know the wet weight of a lens epithelium, but it wasn't much. Nirenberg was asking for literally thousands of samples for every experiment. It would be like chewing a steak the size of a cow.

"I see," said Nirenberg. "Why are you so interested in chicken lens cells? It's such an esoteric biological system. How many people care how a chicken lens cell makes crystallins or how it elongates? The lens cells do elongate as they develop, no?"

"Yes, they do, and they make a ton of crystallins. What would you suggest I study?"

"Viruses. They're very 'hot' now and one can do a lot of experiments. Do you know George Todaro's work? *That's* interesting."

I'd never even heard of Todaro or his research.

"But so many people are working on viruses. It's kind of a crowded field, isn't it?"

"Yes, that's good. Many people will be interested in any little discovery you publish."

Any little discovery I added to the voluminous scientific literature on viruses would be noted! Was that my research goal?

I returned to the lab discouraged, although I appreciated Nirenberg's honesty concerning the technical difficulties and limited audience for my project. I had no idea who would be interested in my research, but I didn't like the idea of galloping to keep abreast with other competitors on similar problems. Chasing an audience and molding my research around the sacred "bandwagon" of the times – what others found interesting – felt unimaginative and derivative, following rather than leading.

As I dissected lens explants that evening, I worried about my future in research, but was proud that few scientists could perform the microsurgery that had taken me months to master. I marveled at the wonder of embryonic development as I gazed into the microscope – the beating heart, the choreography of organ formation that Hoadley called morphochoresis, and the crystal-clear lens. Perhaps I was heading toward a brick wall, but when I peered into the dissecting microscope, the developing eye of the chicken stared back, challenging me to learn its secrets.

That night I accepted that my research on the lens might end as a futile attempt to cast a dim light on a dark shadow. My research might be as invisible as the lens was transparent, but at least it would be my own: an expression of what I wanted to explore. Science wasn't just revealing nature's secrets, it was a form of expression for the scientist as well: what problems were chosen, the elegance of the research, the extrapolations of the conclusions – all art as much as science. Instead of many being interested in each little discovery I might (or might not!) make, a few may be intrigued by something new that I might discover or propose, something that might tempt others to take a peek as well. I dreamed of discovering hidden treasures in the obscure chicken lens, which focused images and magnified spots. Optimism always trumped my pessimism, and dreams tended to take over. My special family stood firmly in the background, tacitly reminding me to keep my eye above the horizon.

The relative simplicity of the lens with its massive expression of a very few genes remained for me potentially like fishing in a small pond stocked with fish. How could I not catch something? I rationalized not to judge the book before it was written, as I had rationalized not to drop science for SocRel in college before I had tried. I continued to dissect into the dark, quiet nights.

Months later I wrote to Harold Barnes, who had become a pen pal after my summer at Millport, venting my frustrations about NIH bureaucracy, discouraged with my research progress, and uncertain about future directions. I received the following response.

"You sound a little depressed with your work," he wrote. "This, of course, is because you tackle BIG problems – with fame and fortune in mind! If only you would do simple things, you would get less frustrated. Now please don't ask what are simple things. At any rate once you are away from your depressing bureaucracy you will probably make rapid progress – unless some other temptation of the more favorable environment intervenes."

As for the bureaucracy, Barnes was right. I would have settled for a handshake instead of the incessant government bureaucracy, however I understood the necessity of bureaucracy to run the immense NIH. As for tackling "simple things," I had no clue what he meant. But the "more favorable environment," that came sooner than I thought.

Lona and I departing for our honeymoon on our wedding day, 1969

Lona and I with Auran (right) and Anton (left), circa 1974.

Auran and Papa in Bethesda, circa 1973.

A More Favorable
Environment

In January 1969, single, almost 29 and in the second year of postdoctoral research, I was ripe to meet the woman of my dreams. Taking pity on my status as a bachelor, fellow scientist at NIH, Ron Goor teamed with his wife Nancy to become a self-appointed 1960s version of a computer dating service.

"Want to meet a great girl?" Ron asked me as I was leaving a science lecture at NIH. "She's here in the audience."

"I can't now, Ronnie. I've got to get home."

"Why?" he asked, looking annoyed.

"Nixon is introducing his cabinet choices on TV in an hour. I would like to watch. How about a rain check?"

That goes down as one of the stupidest choices I've made in my life. I'm not even a Republican!

The rain check came January 12, the day of Super Bowl III, when the New York Jets beat the Baltimore Colts for an enormous upset. I had no idea that another major moment was about to come for me.

Lona opened the door of her efficiency apartment above the garage of Hans Cahnmann, a senior scientist at NIH. She was wearing a green kilt held together with a large chrome pin. I'm amazed how small details can assume disproportionate and lasting importance. It wasn't just the kilt or the pin, of course. It was her brown eyes, her unpretentious manner, her smile. Her small apartment included a large birdcage filled with strawberry finches - their flitting around seemed to welcome me.

Since I was improvising as to how the afternoon would proceed, I asked if she had any interest in watching the Super Bowl.

"What's that?" she said.

Yes! We were on the same wavelength. Though I could have listed the Wimbledon winners without difficulty, I had never even heard of Joe Namath (Broadway Joe) or Johnny Unitas, the famed quarterbacks of the two Super Bowl teams. In fact, I knew very little about football then.

So, it was coffee, not football. We went to the Old Angler's Inn by the Chesapeake and Ohio canal in Potomac. The Super Bowl kept everyone at home watching television and the restaurant deserted. Lona and I sat by the fireplace and drank hot coffee getting acquainted.

This was a perfect storm in reverse: Everything was right, just how it should be.

"You're left-handed," she observed, when I picked up my cup of coffee.

Can you imagine how I felt? A beautiful girl with soft brown eyes, who noticed I was left-handed. Two hours after we met, just as Broadway Joe was becoming a football legend, I started wondering what kind of wife Lona would make.

Not prone to rash decisions, I needed to make sure before proposing.

We talked. Lona said she'd graduated from the University of Chicago in biology, so we had science in common, as well as no interest (yet) in football. She was working as a technician in the Metabolism Branch in the National Cancer Institute, so we had NIH in common too. When I said I had an older sister, she told me she had an older brother, Larry.

"What does he do?" I asked.

"Larry's a physicist in Austin."

A-ha! Another common denominator: an older sibling of the opposite sex, and he was a scientist.

We went back to her apartment and talked some more. I was dead-set against saying goodbye, so I checked what she planned for dinner.

"I have a couple of steaks in the refrigerator," she said, adding that she wanted to try a new recipe involving peanuts from India or Indonesia – one of those.

This sounded risky to me, but I wasn't about to leave.

"Sounds delicious," I said.

I went home reluctantly after midnight.

Our second date set off alarm bells. On our way to the Iron Gate Inn for dinner we stopped at the row house I rented in Georgetown, so I could change out of my work clothes and send a birthday telegram to my grandmother in Paris. In 1969 telegrams were costly versions of today's emails.

"The telegram goes to Baroness Édouard de Roth-schild," I told the Western Union operator.

Lona was paging through a magazine pretending to pay no attention to my call. However, when I hung up she asked, "Does your grandmother live on Rothschild Street?"

"No," I said. "Her name is Rothschild."

"Rothschild, like *the* Rothschilds?"

"Yes."

I suddenly felt vulnerable, as if I wasn't myself any-more. Revealing my Rothschild connection was announcing my wealth, at least to another Jew. Discretion about money was our family rule. I was a scientist and a Piatigorsky as much as a Rothschild grandson. Once again, I felt pressure to sidestep the "rich kid" label – possibly spoiled, both maligned and envied as the beneficiary of privilege.

When I proposed some four months later, the Rothschild connection re-surfaced.

"I don't want to live in a glass house," she said, appearing flustered.

Is that what being a Rothschild grandson meant? Or was it my famous father that she imagined would interfere with her life? Did she really think marrying me would direct a spotlight on her?

We talked.

"Yes," she said after I extinguished that annoying spot-light.

Then I learned of the mysterious six degrees of separation, except make that less than six. Lona's paternal uncle, Abraham Mandel Schechtman, a professor of embryology at UCLA, died of a brain tumor in 1962, and Tyler at nearby Caltech taught his course the following year to help out. Who would believe it? Lona was indirectly connected with my thesis advisor seven years before we even met!

It was even more eerie than that. Lona's uncle couldn't decide whether to go into art or science as a boy. His decision to become a scientist was based in part on the fact that he found no outstanding schools for art when his family settled in Los Angeles. The art-science interplay was represented in Lona's family.

Our match was pre-ordained.

A few weeks after our engagement, my Georgetown neighbors threw a wonderful block party. My rented house was on 26th Street, with a relatively quiet, short residential setting. I had become friends with other residents in a houseful of single women, sometimes dropping in to chill, as they say. They arranged with other neighbors a celebratory dinner for Lona and me, in which we went from house to house for the different courses – a memorable way to end my bachelor days and join the society of married folks!

We planned to have our wedding at the Hotel America in Washington, D.C. and needed a rabbi, but we neither were religious nor belonged to a temple. A neighbor of Lona's parents recommended a friend, Rabbi William Seaman, who arrived at the ceremony wearing tennis shoes, to be able to dash off for his heavy schedule that day. He had squeezed our wedding between a tombstone dedication in the morning and a funeral later in the afternoon. Busy man!

For some, the marriage vow "...until death do us part" is a mere formality that life obscures for one reason or another. For Lona and me, however, marriage was sacred, as significant as we aged as the day we pledged ourselves to each other. Marriage was more than a union for us; it was creating one enriched, expanded life from two, without losing our individuality.

What a lopsided number of family members attended our wedding! My entire family in the United States – my parents, Jephta, her husband Dan and their three boys, all under nine years old – were there, as was my grandmother Babushka and uncle Guy from Paris, and my aunt Bethsabée from Israel.

Babushka, in her late eighties, arrived the day before the wedding. Jet-lagged, she woke up after midnight, confused and disoriented. She dialed random numbers on the telephone by her hotel bed and awoke an assortment of irate guests. That was Lona's first contact with my Rothschild relatives!

In contrast to my few kinfolks, Lona had a basketful, bestowing me suddenly with a large American family, who turned out to be wonderful family members to have. Lona tutored me about who was married and related to whom, their idiosyncrasies, and so on. Lona's mother alone had five siblings, and each had spouses and children. It took me a few years to keep them all straight.

There we were, a married couple in our fancy wedding attire, dancing and in love. That's when the photographer tapped me on the shoulder.

"Excuse me," he said. "I've only been hired until 6 o'clock (we were married at 2 o'clock). I need a picture of you two leaving."

You've got to be kidding, I thought. I'm finally starting to relax and have fun.

"Do you mind?" he said.

Yes, I thought. *I mind.* But Lona's parents had arranged and paid for the photographer, not I, and I was reluctant to say, "No sweat. Charge us overtime."

Lona went to change from her wedding gown into her red getaway dress. We left with much fanfare as the photographer snapped his camera.

We flew to New York en route to a honeymoon in Europe. In New York, a bedraggled-looking woman in the street shouted as we passed, "You will rot in Hell!"

This was not the prophecy I'd hoped for, but a helpful first lesson of married life: don't believe everything you hear.

No marriage can be summarized by a single point of view or event. However, one anecdote reflects how Lona helped me put my identity in perspective. Soon after we were married, we went to a concert by Vladimir Horowitz at the Daughters of the American Revolution hall. I'd never met or heard Horowitz, a colleague of Papa's years earlier, play the piano in person. Horowitz, Nathan Milstein and Papa had played as a trio in Europe when they were young. After the concert, Lona suggested that we go backstage and say hello.

"He would be happy to meet Papa's son," she said.

I balked. I felt an invisible connection to Horowitz via Papa, but at the same time I resisted. I had mixed feelings about going backstage – like being Piatigorsky, but the son.

Lona insisted. "He was Papa's friend."

True. I agreed to go.

We knocked on the door of his dressing room. No response. I was partially relieved and ready to leave, but Lona knocked again, and then again. After some time, the door opened.

"Mr. Horowitz is not receiving guests," said a man abruptly, and shut the door.

Okay, I thought. Let's go home. I knew Horowitz was a recluse.

Lona knocked again, more forcefully. The door opened once more.

"What..." the man started to speak, looking annoyed.

Lona didn't let him finish. "Please tell Mr. Horowitz that Gregor Piatigorsky's son would like to say hello."

The poor man looked bewildered. He left and a few seconds later Horowitz appeared. He couldn't have been more cordial, and seemed happy to meet us. *Fait accompli!* Still, I'm uncomfortable among musicians. I wouldn't want to be anyone else's son, but I also wanted – needed – to be me.

With Lona, my wife, I became me.

One part of me that changed with marriage was religion. I remained an atheist but came more to terms with being an ethnic Jew, which I always was in my heart. I was close to Jephta, whose husband was raised as an orthodox Jew, and so under their influence we started celebrating Chanukah instead of Christmas. We joined a temple, and our boys, Auran and Anton, had a Bar Mitzvah, which I never did, and we went to Temple on the High Holy Days.

Harold Barnes had been right that "temptation of the more favorable environment" would enrich my life at NIH. However, despite Leo Tolstoy's famous opening line in Anna Karenina that "all happy families are alike," even happy families have their unique difficulties.

Of our many positive experiences together – travels, celebrations, mutual friends, the whole grand package of life with its glitters and blemishes – none topped the birth of our two boys. Lona and I became four, and from my perspective that difference was not two but infinity. I regret only that I was not in the delivery room with Lona for the birth of our sons. In the early seventies, it was less common for fathers to be there during birth of their children. The obstetrician never asked me if I wanted to stay with Lona in the delivery room and still under the influence of my European parents where it was not common practice, I never suggested it.

After having two healthy boys 18 months apart, we had another boy on the way. The little fellow kicked Lona's stretched abdomen, ferociously announcing that we'd better prepare for him. But a family of five was not to be. He was born prematurely in the eighth month and died six hours later. Genetic diagnosis was trisomy 13, a rare anomaly of an extra thirteenth chromosome. However, nothing is rare when it happens to you. Lona only saw him briefly in the delivery room; I caught a better glance of him when he was transferred to the nursery before he died. He never had a chance.

While Lona was pregnant, our nameless little boy had already become a strong presence in our family. Auran and Anton expected another sibling and new friend that never came. "It can't happen to you," I told them. "You're here for good."

Our third son never cried at night for Lona's milk; he never felt the comfort of my holding him, or I the miracle of his warm body against mine. His death reduced our family from an expected five to the original four, which is no reduction in fact. Yet, four felt empty. Our third child was missing, our family felt incomplete. Death had stolen what we assumed we had.

I remember sounding so matter-of-fact speaking to the doctor after our poor child died. We didn't know yet the cause of death and speculated it was maybe this or maybe that. Chromosomal anomaly came up as a possibility, which turned out to be the case. The scientist in me camouflaged the human ache inside. Later I realized that my effort to be dispassionate in my research, to interpret data from a distance and not force wishful hopes, also masked my muted passion for what I was doing and hoped to accomplish.

I was who I was, whether at home or in the laboratory.

A year later Lona was pregnant again. Amniocentesis confirmed another boy with a normal chromosomal count. Filled with hope, we bought a larger house, and then his heart stopped beating in the second trimester. Why? Not knowing can be more unsettling than certainty. We never learned the answer.

The boy was dead, it made no difference why; yet he still remained in Lona's body. I shared the heavy death as if it were in my body too, which blended us together in a deeper, human way, but certainly not a happy way. A forced abortion – an agonizing procedure that took several weeks of intravenous hormones – another heartache, another time that death reached out to us.

Our marriage vow, "Until death do us part," had played an unexpected, unwanted role. Not all events are happy in a happy life.

Again, my research comes to mind. How many times hope rose to anticipation, but then came a different truth:

the experiment failed, the idea wrong, only disappointment left. What works outdoes all else; what works is what counts.

Happenstance often shapes destiny despite the careful choices we make to carve our fate. We must play the cards we're dealt. Papa knew this well from his stormy life. Each morning while still in bed, he opened his eyes to make sure that he could see. Then he wiggled his fingers and toes to confirm that they obeyed. Finally, he stood and walked.

"If it all works as expected," he said, "I'm a happy man. There are no guarantees."

That's right, there are no guarantees in life. But there are new opportunities, and they became my focus.

Lona, Anton, Joram and Auran in Cape Cod, 1972.

Optimism and Pipedreams

Newly married, and after two years of being a postdoctoral fellow, it was time to obtain a faculty position. However, I was dissatisfied with my research progress. While I could replicate what Coulombre's lab had shown with the cultured lens explants, although with more detail, I hadn't discovered much new. Nonetheless, apparently having gained some presence due to my attendance at conferences, I was invited to give a lecture at the University of Michigan in Ann Arbor as part of their recruitment effort, which was my first job interview. The lecture went well and the vibrant college environment teeming with students attracted me. NIH seemed lackluster by comparison.

A few weeks later I was offered a position as an assistant professor. Flattered, I was tempted to accept, and consulted Papa for advice.

"Will you have to teach?" he asked.

"Sure," I replied. "It's a university."

"But don't you have to know something before you teach?"

Was he kidding? What was the "something" I needed to know? Hadn't my years at Harvard and Caltech followed by two postdoctoral years at NIH taught me anything? Yet, I didn't reject Papa's indirect advice to stay at NIH if I could arrange it and do research. It was largely what I wanted to do, and Papa's comment may not have been tactful, but it made sense from his perspective, and it targeted my aims. He had risen from the precarious "college of life" and earned success by his virtuosity as a cellist. I wanted demonstrable "virtuosity" as a scientist, and I didn't feel I was anywhere near accomplishing that. Also, why seek Papa's advice if I didn't listen to it? Was I just probing for confirmation?

I declined the offer, but I had no clear path for staying at NIH. Getting on the staff at NIH was as competitive as landing a faculty position at a university. Then fate tumbled in my direction.

A year earlier, Coulombre had become the Scientific Director of the National Institute of Child Health and Human Development (NICHD; the NIH Institute that Tyler had a hand in establishing), and consequently moved his laboratory administratively from the NINDB to the NICHD. Shortly thereafter, he stepped down as Scientific Director and his laboratory returned to the NINDB. I saw this as an opportunity to fill the vacancy left by Coulombre for a developmental biologist at the NICHD. With the same chutzpah I had when I barged in on Albert Tyler at Caltech, I approached Charles Lowe, the newly appointed Scientific Director of NICHD.

"Dr. Coulombre is gone from the NICHD," I said, "so I would like to replace him by starting a laboratory on developmental biology at your Institute." I had not appreciated then the extent to which NIH Laboratory Chiefs had established careers and were leaders in their fields with many publications; they were not ambitious novices. I doubt that a similar request today from someone with as few credentials as I had would receive a second thought. Remarkably, however, Lowe listened to me, as Tyler had a few years earlier.

"Write up what you want," he said. "I'll look it over and see what I think."

That was good enough for me. I wrote a proposal to study sea urchin fertilization, furthering my graduate school research because I knew that best, and to extend my research on lens cell differentiation, a two-pronged approach to study development. I requested a technician, a postdoctoral fellow, and sufficient space to do my research.

Lowe called me to his office a few days after I gave him the proposal. "I can't make you a Laboratory Chief, Joram, but I'm willing to assign a couple of modules (lab rooms) to you, fund a technician and let you do your own research. You would report to me regularly. We'll make this a new appendage – a Developmental Biology Branch – tacked onto the NICHD. I'll act as the Chief, and we'll see how it goes. How's that?"

Pretty amazing! It was courageous and generous of Lowe to give me such independence based on a homemade "grant request." I was impressed how much few decisions made by others who hardly know us can determine our destiny. I hired Sonia Rothschild, who had been Coulombre's technician a few years earlier. Then, Jerome Vinograd, a biophysics professor at Caltech, asked me if I would act as a mentor for Sydney Craig, a "homeless" midstream graduate student stranded by Tyler's death. I agreed. Soon after, Miriam Wollberg, an Israeli technician who accompanied her postdoctoral husband to NIH, joined my laboratory, exceeding Lowe's commitment to fund one technician.

The four of us worked closely side by side under cramped conditions in those formative years. Long days in the laboratory were marked by continual banter on science and other topics. I dissected embryonic lenses while Sonia and Miriam worked steadily to process the cultured cells for histology, and Syd labored to complete his thesis on sea urchin eggs. A sense of camaraderie existed that unfortunately is often lost in larger laboratories. Silly jokes – nonsense – often touched on larger issues that fermented in my mind. I remember when Syd broke the silence of a busy day and asked, "Are you going to work on six-day-old embryonic chicken lenses forever?" (I chose to study the six-day-old embryonic lens because it was large enough to dissect and the epithelial cells differentiated well in culture.)

Syd was serious and I thought his question deserved an answer. "Well, I'm going to study the seven-day-old embryonic chicken lens someday." (Chickens hatch after twenty-one days of development.)

He laughed, but my answer bounced around in my mind. I wondered how cells taken later in development would behave in culture. These musings resulted in a new research project in which Sonia and I charted the gradual loss of developmental potential of the lens cells in culture when taken from older embryos.

Other fanciful questions flowed through my mind as a result of Syd's question that would not occur to overly busy scientists running a larger laboratory. I wondered what was the embryonic age of the explanted lens cells after culture. Were they still six days old, the age at which I removed them from the embryo, or eight days old after forty-eight hours of culture? In other words, did developmental time arrest or reset when the embryonic cells were placed in culture, and if so, how did this regulation of gene expression occur? What relevance might this have to aging in general? Did it make sense to divide different compartments of an embryo into separate time zones at different stages of their differentiation? These thoughts didn't materialize into specific research projects, but I remember such exchanges as valuable for teaching me the importance of disciplining creative ideas, and not to confine a restless mind from meandering or to be overly cautious about making mistakes – better to crystallize ideas into realistic research questions, whether or not they will pan out.

My first publication on the lens wasn't until 1971, two years after I had established the "acting" laboratory of developmental biology, and four years after starting to work on the lens for the first time, a long hiatus that reflected the difficulty of attempting molecular studies on the tiny embryonic lens epithelia before the appropriate technology was available.(21)

As time went by, I recruited Donald Slater, a scientist who worked off campus on sea urchin embryos, and Michael Cashel, a bacteriologist in NINBD, to join our acting Developmental Biology Branch. Lowe added Lon White, a virologist, who worked in still another building, creating a potpourri of bedfellows working on unrelated projects.

When we met together in Lowe's office once a month, I had a sense of being in Hoadley's office, where freewheeling ideas were tossed around. Lowe provided the shield we needed to continue our independent research. Such an atypical opportunity to develop my career was rare. I was lucky. Young investigators free to make choices, to fail and try again, are the foundation and guts of basic science.

As my research advanced I was confronted with a common dilemma. Research questions typically comprise, unwittingly, multiple interconnected problems that confound which ones to follow. For example, I had discovered that insulin treatment of the cultured lens explants promoted both cell elongation (a sign of lens cell differentiation) and the assembly of microtubules in the cells.(22) Microtubules had already been implicated in causing other cells to change shape by previous investigators, making my finding, at best, consistent with a prevailing idea at the time. I didn't know whether to pursue the relation-ship of microtubule assembly and cell elongation, a general area involving the biochemistry of microtubule assembly being investigated by a number of researchers in different tissues, or to switch and concentrate on crystallin synthesis, which defines the lens. Not following up on microtubule assembly seemed like a missed opportunity; however, hopping from one phenomenon (microtubule assembly) to another (crystallin synthesis) seemed superficial. What to do?

At approximately this stage I attended the annual meeting of the American Society of Cell Biology, where I received my first bitter taste of the hardcore profession of science. The meeting bustled with activity: scientists scooted from one room to another to hear scheduled talks. Small groups huddled discussing the latest news filtering through the grapevine. Individuals sat at small tables in the hallways sipping coffee or making last-minute changes for their presentations. Young scientists like myself mixed with university professors and esteemed winners of coveted research prizes. My dreams collided with the daunting challenges of the competitive nature of a science career. I felt like a kid at the beach, anxious to swim, my big toe in the chilly water, but confronted by powerful waves and undertow. I didn't even think of the sharks.

I was scheduled to present my discovery linking insulin treatment, microtubule assembly and lens cell elongation at one of the sessions of the conference. There was standing room only for the presentation before mine. Beth Burnside, an eloquent scientist from the University of California at Berkeley, showed dazzling electron micrographs of micro-tubules in the fish retina. My anxiety rose meteorically during her presentation, since my data lacked the quality of hers, my scientific story was not as rigorous as hers, and my specific plans for future research were still a blur. After a well -deserved round of applause, she answered questions artfully. But when she stepped down – oh my! – the audience filed out, leaving only a few scientists under a blanket of silence.

I walked to the front of the largely empty conference room and delivered my talk listlessly, boring myself as much as I must have the few stragglers left. My science was not up to par, not sufficiently innovative, nothing special. I stood behind the podium berating myself, ignoring whatever qualities my talk might have had. Feeling defeated in my hotel room that evening, I wondered what propelled me to become a scientist.

After that experience, I decided to investigate crystallins, which defined the lens at the genetic and protein levels. Microtubules were in every tissue, thus there was no advantage to study them in the lens. My first focus would be delta-crystallin, since I had already started to characterize it in chickens. Delta-crystallin existed only in bird and reptile lenses, not in human or other vertebrate lenses. I wasn't sure if that was an advantage or disadvantage, since it attracted scant attention, minimizing competition, but allowed me to work at my own pace. There were also other crystallins – for example, alpha-crystallin and beta-crystallin. These were at low concentration in the chicken lens, but abundant in the lenses of other vertebrates. Gamma-crystallin was still another crystallin in most vertebrate lenses. Why such diversity in lens crystallins, when the structure, transparency and function of all lenses was quite similar? Other specialized tissues used similar proteins for comparable functions, such as hemoglobin in red blood cells for example. A fascinating world of complexity and opportunity lay before me.

Focusing on crystallins gave me the research direction I needed. The years of floundering; staring into a microscope for hours on end; mastering the art of micro-dissection; attempting molecular biology research on minuscule tissues before the explosion of molecular genetics made it possible to do so; being influenced by Tyler's ideas rather than my own; weathering Nirenberg's suggestion that I study viruses because even a minor finding would interest other scientists;

feeling crushed by scientists walking out of my presentation even before it started, and discouraged by giving less than stellar presentations at conferences. Being uncertain whether I had blundered into science without the talent to be a scientist had come to an end.

I had a long-term strategy for my research. In addition, the age of recombinant DNA and molecular cloning, still in its infancy, suggested exciting promise for new approaches to study genes. The quicksand under my feet was solidifying.

Again, fate, nudged by Lowe, tumbled in my direction.

In 1971 Philip Leder, an eminent NIH scientist who had been a postdoctoral fellow with Marshal Nirenberg and a pioneer in molecular genetics was establishing a new NICHD laboratory, the Laboratory of Molecular Genetics. Lowe, ready to dissolve my maverick Developmental Biology Branch, asked Leder if he would consider letting me join his laboratory. A few days later, Leder interviewed me. After I told him about my research on the eye lens, we had the following brief exchange:

"Okay, Joram, I think it would be fine to have you join my laboratory," he said.

"That would be wonderful," I responded. "I would learn a great deal and greatly enlarge the scope of my work."

Suddenly worried whether I could hold my own in this high-powered group, I asked, "But what could I contribute?"

He paused. "You would provide intellectual stimulation without threatening anyone."

I had no intention of threatening anyone! But Leder's comment made sense in view of the competitive nature of science. My challenge was to guard myself against feeling threatened by the high-powered scientists that were about to become my colleagues.

I became a member of Leder's Laboratory of Molecular Genetics, along with Michael Cashel, a colleague in our transient Developmental Biology Branch. I hired a small group of postdoctoral fellows to conduct research on the crystallins. By 1976 I had become a credible molecular biologist and the Head of the Section on Cellular Differentiation, one of the five independent research groups in Leder's laboratory.

Recombinant DNA technology promoted an alternate way of thinking: targeting the gene to understand the lens, rather than analyzing the lens to understand gene expression. More generally, reductionism to study the parts could be used to reconstruct the whole. Leder's laboratory gave me an opportunity to redefine the crystallins in terms of their genes, to study how the crystallin genes are regulated (turned on and off) during development, and to trace their evolution by comparative analysis of different species. I had a realistic agenda for an indeterminate number of years in an overwhelming playground of enormous complexity. Pipedreams sang a new tune. However, while the possibility of tapping genes directly was inspiring, mastering molecular biology to do so seemed as difficult as becoming a virtuoso musician without knowing the fingerings to play the music on a new instrument. The task sent me back to kindergarten.

I had obtained a great deal of information on chicken delta-crystallin, including a hint that two genes might encode it. Suraj Bhat, a new postdoctoral fellow in my

Section, was anxious to clone these genes from the mass of chicken DNA, a technology analogous to finding a specific hair in a flock of sheep. Cloning was a two-step process. First, the delta-crystallin messenger RNA for the gene had to be converted to a complementary DNA (cDNA) and then cloned, which meant replicating it thousands of times by growing it in bacteria. The cloned cDNA could then be used essentially as "bait" to fish out and subsequently clone the delta-crystallin genes. Cloning delta-crystallin was analogous to detective work: the guilty gene (delta-crystallin) needed to be located (identified in the total genome, the job of the cDNA), arrested and replicated (cloned), and interrogated (sequenced). In addition to cloning and determining the structures of delta-crystallin and other crystallin genes, my goal was to bring attention to the largely ignored lens and crystallins – put them at the cutting edge of research in molecular biology.

Although such molecular cloning was going on in Leder's laboratory, it was another thing for us to accomplish it ourselves. Suraj followed existing protocols carefully, but met with repeated failures. Looking discouraged after he had drained the tube that contained the delta-crystallin messenger RNA without success to start the cloning process, he said, "Nothing works, Joram. What to do?"

"I guess you'll need to obtain more delta-crystallin messenger RNA and start from scratch. I know it's a lot of work," I said, willing to help him with the time-consuming collection of literally thousands of embryonic chicken lenses that were required to get enough messenger RNA to start the cloning process again. I remembered the heartbreak when Peggy Zelenka, a postdoctoral fellow at the time, and I spent grueling days dissecting embryonic chicken lenses on our first effort to have enough delta-crystallin messenger RNA for our experiments on crystallin synthesis before the cloning era, only to lose much of it when a centrifuge tube collapsed during the purification process. Research demands stamina!

Suddenly, Suraj perked up.

"Some delta-crystallin cDNA has to be still in the original test tube," he said. "I know it's there. I'll find a way to clone it."

"How's that possible, Suraj? The tube's empty. There's nothing left to work with."

"I'll bet there's some cDNA stuck to the plastic. I'll add water, swirl and clone it!"

I let it go at that.

He added water to the tube, swirled as he'd said to free whatever might have been clinging to the sides of the tube and repeated the cloning protocol. Amazingly, Suraj obtained one lonely cDNA clone. One! He'd done it! That started the whole field of cloning crystallin genes for us, as well for other laboratories working on crystallins, and changed the direction of our research for years. We were in business.(23)

Suraj's persistence portrayed the importance of optimism in research, even at times a refusal to accept failure that borders on being stubborn or foolish. Pessimism in research often becomes a self-inflicted destiny. Laboratory research can be like trying to keep your balance on a tightrope. It's neither for the fainthearted nor a pessimist.

Suraj went on with Ray Jones, another postdoctoral fellow, to identify and clone two delta-crystallin genes from the chicken.(24) Each gene had seventeen introns (derived from the term 'intragenic regions', meaning interruptions in the continuity of the DNA sequences that code for the protein). The delta-crystallin genes turned out to be the most complex genes known at the time, when relatively few genes had been cloned. Although larger and more complex genes were identified in other laboratories soon thereafter, the delta-crystallin genes are still the most structurally complex crystallin genes.

Such molecular analysis and gene cloning might be compared to splitting the atom and identifying its elementary particles. DNA cloning provided invaluable new insights about genetics that promised applications in the future. Examples popular at the time include repairing defective genes, boosting agricultural harvests, and modifying bacteria to mop up oil spills. The ultimate benefits were incalculable and depended on imagination and resources. I couldn't have been in a better place at the time than in Leder's lab – a center of the burgeoning field of molecular genetics well supported by the government – and having the time to focus on research.

We were on the way to a molecular description of crystallins and their genes when my productive home in Leder's laboratory suddenly dissolved.

.

Philip Leder at a luncheon before he left the National Institutes of Health to establish the Department of Genetics at Harvard Medical School and occupy the John Emory Andrus Chair, 1980.

Free to Make Mistakes

In 1980, Leder left NIH to head the Department of Genetics at Harvard Medical School, leaving my future at NIH uncertain. The enormous resources at NIH – one of the most coveted and scientifically productive research institutions worldwide – made it a paradise for research. Superb scientists willing to collaborate and share knowledge and equipment populated the campus, and government funding obviated the loss of time and uncertainty of obtaining grants. Also, the privilege of being able to follow scientific leads and not be shackled by earlier commitments made in grant proposals gave invaluable academic freedom, akin to meandering through a dense forest, testing one way and then another, until spotting a possible clearing to advance a few steps. Occasionally, a fundamental discovery is made by chance colliding with a receptive mind. It is the dream of every basic scientist to stumble into such a green pasture.

An opportunity to establish my own laboratory at NIH came in 1981, when Leder went to Harvard and Jin Kinoshita was appointed Scientific Director of the National Eye Institute (NEI).

Kinoshita and I investigated the eye lens, worked in the same building and had co-authored an article on crystallin synthesis. Aware that I needed a new scientific home, Kinoshita offered me the opportunity to establish a laboratory on molecular biology in the NEI. At first this seemed perfect, but then I fretted that being a laboratory chief – the NIH equivalent of a department chairperson in academia – would load me with bureaucracy and distance me from the heart of science. I was also concerned that the NEI might be too specialized on the eye for my general interests in basic science. I sought the advice of J. Edward Rall, the Deputy Scientific Director of NIH, who had a broad view of science.

"Do it," said Rall. "The NEI needs a laboratory on molecular biology. It's clearly the road to the future." He assured me that the NEI Director, Carl Kupfer, would be supportive. He also gave me a peculiar warning.

"Just remember one thing, Joram," he said at the end of our discussion. "Not everything works." That was it. No explanation, no examples from his own experiences.

"Expect failures. What works is what counts."

Having no idea of what might or might not work, I proposed to establish the Laboratory of Molecular and Developmental Biology (LMDB) in the NEI and negotiated space, funded positions and the like with Kupfer and Kinoshita. My plan was that the laboratory would have several interacting sections with complementary research projects, some more medically oriented and some more basic in nature. My own group – the Section on Molecular Biology – would focus on the eye lens, stressing basic principles in genetics, development and evolution. The deal was sealed when Kupfer didn't balk at my final, unusual request.

"When I make mistakes," I said, thinking of Rall's caution in different terms, "and no doubt I will make a number, I want the freedom to make important mistakes."

I thought trivial mistakes were hardly a source of significant growth, but important mistakes could be a prologue to what works.

"Okay," he said. From one moment to the next I had the responsibility for creating a productive environment that makes meaningful scientific contributions and trains future scientists. There would be no one to blame for failure but myself. That had always been the case, but now it was in neon lights.

The day after I signed a contract that established the LMDB, I gave Jin Kinoshita a bottle of champagne and said, "Here's to an exciting new beginning."

Kinoshita looked surprised, but pleased, and then he said, "Joram, would you do me a favor?"

What did he want from me already?

Kinoshita continued in all seriousness, "I would appreciate if you could have at least half of your research connected with the eye. I need to justify the work to Congress, who funds us."

Taken aback, I suddenly realized that he was as concerned that my interests might be too broad for the NEI as I was that the NEI's interests might be too limited for me.

"*All* of my research will have relevance for the eye, even if some projects don't use eye tissues," I said.

Eye biology was no different from any other biology. It was universal, like the genetic code. There was no reason for concern. Jin smiled. He was broad-minded and truly appreciated basic science. We were on the same wavelength.

Realizing my lifelong dream of having my own laboratory was a milestone in my life. However, the cliché – be careful what you wish for because you may get it – worried me. Being a laboratory chief meant being responsible for several independent sections with numerous postdoctoral fellows and technicians. As I feared when seeking advice from Rall, being a laboratory chief brought a barrage of bureaucracy and the constant need to continue and expand support for the laboratory. My crystal ball showed me increasingly confined to my office under a mound of responsibilities. There was good reason to bypass such an "honor." I didn't want my dream to become a nightmare. However, if I weren't the laboratory chief, if I remained in someone else's laboratory, I would be a part of someone else's overall vision. I preferred the challenge of directing my own fate.

Accepting being a laboratory chief, reminded me of an earlier conversation I had had with my colleague Bob Crouch, a biochemist in Leder's laboratory.

"Bob," I said, "when I accomplish any goal that I set for myself, large or small, it never feels as wonderful as my dream for reaching it had. Reality just doesn't match up to the dream. What do you think about that?"

Bob nodded but remained silent.

"When a dream comes true," I continued, searching for an answer to my question, "I guess I need to dream another dream."

Of course! Dreams were mirages, but without them life would be bland, at least for me. I'd conflated fantasy – dreams – with reality for as long as I could remember:

dreams of winning tennis victories at Wimbledon when I was a teenager, which spurred me on to play better tennis, and dreams of discoveries as a scientist, which kept me optimistic in my research. New dreams were antidotes to the realities that glittered less than their promises. Now my dream for my own laboratory needed to be translated to specific goals: define the crystallins in terms of their genes, determine how crystallin genes are regulated during development, probe crystallin gene evolution to complete an image from past to present, and build a thriving intellectual, creative scientific environment.

One caveat must be added: I knew I sacrificed continuity beyond myself by devoting my efforts to building a government laboratory. I would have unprecedented (for me) opportunities for research that would be well supported. However, once I retired from NIH, the Scientific Director would certainly replace my laboratory with entirely new laboratories with different missions and different philosophies. My contributions, whatever they might be, would be documented in my publications, but not in a lasting organization that I had established. I settled for that compromise, accepting that nothing lasts forever, to have the advantages of a life of uninterrupted research.

My family had left me confident that nothing was impossible, but my experiences told me that every step was a challenge. Thus, I fluctuated between optimism and realism, my moods mimicking the peaks and valleys of scientific research, where the occasional satisfactions – the rare times when experiments succeeded – sustained the disappointments.

Bob Crouch and I gossiped once about various high-profile scientists, including Leder.

"Leder's passionate about science. He's intense - driven," said Bob.

This time it was my turn to nod without comment, preoccupied with thoughts of my own ambition.

Bob continued. "You're entirely different," he said.

"Different? How so?"

"You're laid back, you do science because you like it. It's not the same."

Suddenly I was thrown back to the days when science was an abstraction romanticized by Papa, and when I was a teenage tennis player competing in Southern California. I recalled the time I played against Carl Earn, a professional with a vicious topspin forehand, on Kirk Douglas's home tennis court where Earn taught on occasion. I had never met the famous movie actor. During the match, Douglas emerged from his house and, distracted, I missed an easy volley at the net. Douglas said to Earn, as if I wasn't there, "The kid won't make it. He isn't hungry enough." And then he left. I never saw him again, but I never forgot what he said. It stung.

Some twenty-five years later at NIH, Bob Crouch added that I was "laid back" to Kirk Douglas's comment that I wasn't "hungry enough." Was I "not hungry enough" or too "laid back" to fulfill my ambitions? Did those labels correspond to having had a too secure, too "soft" life – too comfortable to struggle for achievements?

I'm cruising in the mangrove swamp of La Parguera, Puerto
Rico on a jellyfish collecting trip, 1985.

My colleague Joseph Horwitz in his UCLA laboratory, circa 2017.

With Jin Kinoshita at the Jin H. Kinoshita International Symposium in New York, 1989.

No Small Problems

At the first meeting of my fledgling laboratory, nine of us, who included four future heads of independent research groups – Gabriel Vogeli, a new recruit from the National Cancer Institute; Toshimichi (Toshi) Shinohara, my former postdoctoral fellow and colleague; Peggy Zelenka, my first postdoctoral fellow; and I – sat around a table in the conference room staring at one another. I was excited, but scared.

Originally, I'd considered a life in science an idealistic journey – a creative bubble. Now I was confronted with the reality that science, like any other profession, was also a business. I no longer had the benefit of Leder's reputation and network. I felt promoted to primary school and a mere pebble on the beach. It wasn't a question of having some things not work, as Rall had warned me, or making important mistakes, as I'd said to Kupfer: I felt the pressure to survive in the competitive world of research.

Soon after my laboratory had launched multiple research projects, Toshi Shinohara told me that Kinoshita, without consulting me, had asked him if he would like to transfer to Bob Nussenblatt's laboratory, since Toshi was investigating autoimmunity at the time, which seemed to

Kinoshita a better fit for Nussenblatt's Laboratory of Immunology.

"What should I do?" Toshi asked me.

I wanted him to stay in my laboratory, which needed diversity to gain a foothold in the scientific community, and I believed cross-fertilization of related fields a major source of creativity. Moreover, Toshi and I were friends and colleagues and had published a number of articles together. I didn't want to lose a colleague or to see my laboratory diminished, and certainly not before it had gained traction.

I felt undermined by Kinoshita when he had offered Toshi another position without consulting me first.

Although Kinoshita was in charge of the intramural program, I called and told him outright, politely, that it was impossible for me to have authority if he took it upon himself to reorganize my laboratory behind my back. I worried that he would be angry, but he wasn't. He apologized, said I was correct and he wouldn't do it again. Toshi stayed in my laboratory for many years before he left for a position at Harvard Medical School and, ultimately, a professorship at the University of Nebraska Medical Center. There never was any question that Kinoshita was the Scientific Director guiding the NEI as a whole, as a Dean would in a university setting. But after our discussion, there remained no doubt that he respected my position as chief of my laboratory and acted with utmost discretion and consideration. He was a model of good leadership: mutual respect to all individuals regardless of hierarchy.

I modeled my laboratory after that of Leder's, which encouraged exchange of information, had regular meetings to discuss current research (the data club), and had a rigorous journal club to keep abreast of new developments. The scientist/artist streak in me felt comfortable in such an academic environment. Individuals interacting and influencing each other, whether in science or art, drive creativity.

The data clubs served as valuable critiques of our respective projects and kept everyone informed of ongoing work. When scientists from other laboratories got wind of the data club meetings, they asked if they could participate. At first, I agreed – why not deepen the critiques? It turned out, however, that the presence of outside senior scientists inhibited a few of the postdoctoral fellows from presenting unfinished work and from participating in group discussions, as they were uncomfortable asking questions that might seem foolish (but never were). My popularity dropped in the NEI when I decided that our data club had to remain strictly within our laboratory.

"We need a home where we're all free to test ideas, whether right or wrong, as we try to advance our work," I said to those who may have been disappointed to stop coming.

Kupfer called me when he heard that I had confined the data club to my laboratory. "What's going on, Joram? Why did you limit attendance to your laboratory's data club? You're a resource to the NEI."

That the NEI Director thought my laboratory a resource flattered me, but it didn't change my mind. I told him the enlarged data club changed the family atmosphere in which preliminary results and problems were discussed freely. I don't think he agreed with me. Nonetheless, I held firm and all the postdoctoral fellows, once again, participated more actively in the discussions.

As in Leder's laboratory, no one, from beginning postdoctoral fellows to Section Heads, including myself, was exempt from the mandatory journal club. The presenters rotated alphabetically on a regular schedule and gave an hour talk; that changed to two half-hour presentations when the laboratory became much larger. The journal club occurred first thing in the morning once a month, and the speaker had the responsibility of bringing doughnuts or bagels for everyone. That ensured that no one could disappoint the group by claiming they forgot it was their turn.

I considered the journal club as important for each member of the laboratory as the data club. Journal clubs are often first on the chopping block, like art in government-funded priorities, but that is no measure of their importance, in my opinion. Recognizing what's useful and interesting in the deluge of new publications was vital training for researchers at all levels. Each speaker wrote a brief synopsis of his or her presentation. I spent many hours choosing and writing up the topics I presented. Although a burden on my time, it was always a learning experience.

One more word about conducting journal clubs: I joined a NIH-wide journal club in the general area of embryonic development that included about a dozen scientists from different Institutes. Since development is a broad area, I suggested after the first year that we might focus on a mutually agreed topic of development, and this was adopted the following year. After a couple of sessions, fewer people attended, interest waned, and the journal club soon disbanded. Perhaps the journal club had simply run its course, but I think there was an important lesson to learn: restricting freedom – limiting presentations at the expense of what arouses personal interest at the moment – was counterproductive to a creative environment.

I insisted on a summer break from our data and journal clubs from July 4 until after Labor Day in September, which allowed uninterrupted focus on research as well as the freedom to take a guiltless vacation without interrupting schedules. I strongly believed that leisure and some distance from routine provided important space where creative ideas could percolate.

The laboratory grew in numbers and visibility as our output increased, and I was proud of its dynamic atmosphere. When I went to the laboratory after dinner or on a weekend, there were generally individuals at work on their projects. This reminded me of a conversation I had years earlier with a scientific director during my postdoctoral days. I had read that postdoctoral scientists in the Department of Agriculture were paid more than those at NIH at the time.

"Why is that?" I asked. "I thought NIH was the most prestigious research facility of the government. Why would we be paid less?"

"Oh, that's easy to answer," said the Scientific Director. "Do you work nights or weekends?"

"Yes, often," I replied.

"Do you receive overtime?"

"No. That never crossed my mind."

"See! We get you guys for nothing."

He was kidding to a certain extent, but also hit upon a kernel of truth. We were passionate about science and completely devoted to our research. Total commitment was always my first criterion for accepting a prospective postdoctoral fellow in my laboratory. I had little patience for those who considered research a stepping-stone to something he or she might consider higher. Our overtime was the privilege to work overtime.

It was the research that preoccupied me.

Once we had cloned a number of crystallin genes, we turned our attention to how the gene for alphaA-crystallin was expressed so specifically in the mouse lens and no other tissue (or so we thought at the time) during development. Ana Chepelinsky, a senior scientist in my laboratory, had discovered a small stretch of DNA (called a promoter) in front of the gene that accounted for its expression.(25) This was our first firm foothold to investigate the regulation of a crystallin gene.

We collaborated with Heiner Westphal, one of the section leaders in Leder's laboratory, to produce transgenic mice (mice containing foreign genes introduced experimentally), which was the most rigorous method to test for promoter activity (gene expression) in the developing embryo at the time. Transgenic mice were made by injecting fertilized eggs with a recombinant gene consisting of the crystallin gene promoter attached to a bacterial gene that encoded an easily monitored product; the injected egg containing the recombinant gene was implanted into a surrogate female mouse and allowed to develop. We detected that the small DNA switch – the promoter – activated the recombinant gene only in the lens.(26) It was analogous to a light switch that worked only in a specific room and nowhere else.

Ana developed a temporary transgenic mouse facility, so we could produce our own transgenic mice; however, I wanted to set up a permanent facility in order to have the capacity to do an extensive series of experiments. Eric Wawrousek, a former postdoctoral fellow in my laboratory, had become an expert in this area at Smith, Kline and French, where he worked. Perfect, I thought. Perhaps he'll set-up a transgenic facility for us. He was interested when I called him, but there was a bureaucratic problem: NIH couldn't match his industrial salary due to restrictive government guidelines. A few days later around six o'clock, I was in the laboratory when I received a phone call from the personnel office.

"Joram, we can't find a way to overcome our government rules to get Eric here. Do you think you might speak to Ed Rall? We understand you know him."

"It's a long shot," I said, "but I'll try."

Although past normal working hours, I called Rall, who was still in his office, and asked if he had time to speak to me about a problem.

"Sure, Joram. Come on over."

What a breath of fresh air, to have the phone answered on the first ring after hours, no secretary and no voicemail – just Ed. I went immediately to his office and saw a book on marine invertebrates on his desk. I took this as a good omen – an open-minded physician, an eminent endocrinologist specializing on thyroid, and deputy director of the NIH, interested in marine invertebrates.

After we greeted each other and before I said a word about Eric, Ed said, "Okay, Joram, you've twisted my arm."

What was he talking about?

"We'll get Wawrousek here. The transgenic facility is important."

Clearly, the personnel office had already approached Rall, however apparently unable to get him to bend the rigid rules. Now, Ed Rall had helped me once before, the first time with advice, this time with getting Eric Wawrousek hired. Eric established a transgenic mouse facility in my lab that led to the identification of a number of control switches for different crystallin genes. I fought for the facility being a part of my laboratory; that would keep Wawrousek engaged in research and abreast of the rapid advances in science, rather than become purely a technical service. I had to appease fears that we would monopolize his services by guaranteeing that the facility would function on a first come basis to serve everyone in the NEI equally, which it did. The facility never showed preference for our experiments over anyone else's and made many notable research contributions.

Our cloning experiments, and those of other laboratories, were redefining the lens crystallins in terms of their amino acid sequences, gene structures and gene control elements, as we had hoped. Our crystallin research had proved Santiago Raman y Cajal, winner of the 1906 Nobel

Prize, correct when he said in his famous book, *Advice for a Young Investigator,* "There are no small problems. Problems that appear small are large problems that are not understood." *(27)*

We had turned the corner; crystallins had appeared to be a "small problem" confined to the lens, but now was recognized as a "large problem" of gene expression. The lens and crystallins attracted wide attention and were directly relevant to studies on genetics, development, evolution, and the growing interests in genetic engineering.

A startling discovery we had not anticipated, however, highlighted the crystallins even further and put them on the world stage of science.

With J. Edward Rall before I gave the 1991 G. Burroughs Mider Lecture at the National Institutes of Health.

A Bigger Stage

When I started eye research, the crystallins were correctly assumed to be responsible for making the lens transparent (crystal clear) and able to bend transmitted light to create a focused image on the retina. That was what crystallins did – provide the optical properties of the lens. Crystallins virtually defined the clear lens. If a trace of a crystallin was found outside of the lens, which happened from time to time, it was considered either an error of interpretation, such as cross-reaction by a different protein with immunological similarity, or insignificant leakage, mere biochemical noise. The name crystallin was synonymous with lens.

A personal experience when I visited my son Anton and his family in Canada made me appreciate the extent that names profoundly influence the way we see the world. I went out at night with Anton's father-in-law, Stephen, to view the night sky peppered with brilliant stars. The sheer beauty of the flickering lights in the vast universe overwhelmed me. Then Stephen told me where to aim my binoculars and told me the names of the stars and formations and galaxies that I was looking at. The sky became ordered in my mind, twinkling stars became identified and were no longer random beauty.

Names – just words – defined the sky, created boundaries and structured my thinking about the vast, sparkling universe.

Blind and deaf Helen Keller, only 23 years old, wrote famously in her autobiography, *The Story of My Life*, how her genius teacher, Ann Sullivan, guided her to understand the importance of names and labels.

"We walked down the path to the well-house, attracted by the fragrance of the honeysuckle with which it was covered. Someone was drawing water and my teacher placed my hand under the spout. As the cool stream gushed over one hand she spelled into the other the word water, first slowly, then rapidly. I stood still, my whole attention fixed upon the motions of her fingers. Suddenly I felt a misty consciousness as of something forgotten – a thrill of returning thought; and somehow the mystery of language was revealed to me. I knew then that "w-a-t-e-r" meant the wonderful cool something that was flowing over my hand. That living word awakened my soul, gave it light, hope, joy, set it free! There were barriers still, it is true, but barriers that could in time be swept away.

"I left the well-house eager to learn. Everything had a name, and each name gave birth to a new thought."(28)

Once water had a name, I doubt that Helen Keller ever mistook it for wood. The properties of water were linked to the word spelled on her hand. "W-a-t-e-r" was water and nothing else in her mind.

Similarly, the names of proteins are invariably linked to specialized roles often associated with specific tissues, such as hemoglobin in red blood cells for transporting oxygen sustaining life, or rhodopsin in the retina transforming light to vision. While names identified proteins, they also imprisoned them to assigned tasks. Specialization associated with confinement was easily accepted, since we ordered our lives by the same principle: doctors treated illness, lawyers solved legal problems, barbers cut hair. Naming the profession identified and confined the professional to that career.

A report in 1982 jolted the crystallin field by complicating the influence of names on protein functions.*(29)* Ingolia and Craig showed that a protein in flies named for its function – heat shock protein, because it protected other proteins from excessive heat – had a sequence similar to alpha-crystallin in the lens. Good grief! An alpha-crystallin-like protein in flies, which lacked lenses, had a function completely different from alpha-crystallin's optical function in the lens. Heresy!

Was alpha-crystallin also able to protect proteins like heat shock protein did? My colleague, Joseph Horwitz, at the Jules Stein Eye Institute at UCLA, answered the question: Yes! His experiments showed that mouse alpha-crystallin could function as a heat shock protein.*(30)*

Alpha-crystallin had two functions for the price of one: in addition to its optical functions, it also protected against excessive heat.

Graeme Wistow in my laboratory then found that a major crystallin in the duck lens was an enzyme (protein responsible for metabolism); subsequently we and other laboratories showed that diverse crystallins in various species were also enzymes found at low concentration in tissues throughout the body as well as at high concentration in the lens. We called these double-duty crystallins "enzyme-crystallins" to denote that they carried out both optical and metabolic functions. Further studies showed that in every case the identical gene produced the lens crystallin and the metabolic enzyme. This proved that the crystallin and the enzyme were the very same protein: one gene made one protein with at least two entirely different functions. *(31) (32)*

Although the hundred-year-old belief that the crystallins were as specialized for conferring optical properties as hemoglobin was for transporting oxygen, or as rhodopsin was for vision, might still have been true for those proteins, the unexpected discoveries of alpha-crystallin as a heat shock protein and of other crystallins being enzymes, contradicted the notion that proteins specialized for only one function. I generalized this phenomenon of dual functions by calling it "gene sharing," meaning that two (or more) functions could share the same gene.*(33)*

Often, I was asked why I used the term gene sharing rather than protein sharing, since it was the protein that had two functions. The reason was that proteins are often modified in various ways, so if the crystallin protein was biochemically or structurally changed in any way, it would no longer be identical to the unmodified version. This made the term protein sharing ambiguous. A modified protein isn't identical to its unmodified counterpart. A modified protein, however, still shares the same gene as its unmodified version, making the term gene sharing technically correct. The gene is the common denominator to both functions of its protein product. In addition, gene sharing called attention to the gene rather than the protein. This was important because it implied that expressing a gene in different tissues or at different intensities – modifying the regulation of the gene – was sufficient to elicit a new function for its encoded protein, an idea consistent with additional experiments. The concept of determining protein function by changing gene regulation differed vastly from the prevailing view that genetic mutations were necessary to evolve a new protein function.

Crystallins had upset the belief that specialization confined the biochemical roles of a protein. But the question remained: how extensive was gene sharing? Did invertebrate lenses have enzyme-crystallins?

Picture of me with my arm in front of Papa's picture, circa 1976.

Spineless Creatures

Invertebrates include numerous spineless creatures with imaginative shapes, stunning colors and peculiar lifestyles – such as termites, spiders, snails, sea urchins, squids and many more species. They are foreign to us and look nothing like us. We have no qualms about smashing a clam, or swatting a bothersome fly w ith r olled u p n ewspaper, o r piercing an earthworm on a hook as bait for fish. Corals and sea pens even look like plants, and many believe they are. But invertebrates are animals, and despite their alien appearance, have populated Earth longer than vertebrates.

Many of them have eyes.

Compound eyes of insects, especially of the fruit fly, have been studied in detail. Unlike complex eyes of vertebrates, also known as camera-type eyes with a single lens to focus images on the retina, compound eyes have many surface, tube-like structures (called ommatidia) that guide light to a few photoreceptor cells. Many invertebrates also have small eyes with a transparent lens, which are called either simple eyes or ocelli. Ocelli show resemblances to camera-type eyes. Even flies, w hich h ave c ompound e yes, also have an ocellus on top of their head that alerts the settled fly to evade the swatter before it hits its mark. It is surprising that the lens-containing ocelli have attracted much less attention than the compound eye that differs greatly from our own camera-type eye.

In addition to being curious about ocelli for the sake of knowledge alone, I wanted to determine what crystallins might be in their lenses. Were they the same as those in vertebrates? Did invertebrate ocelli have enzyme-crystallins? Did gene sharing exist in invertebrate lenses?

Investigating invertebrate eyes also had a maverick tone that distinguished me from the overwhelming majority of vision scientists, who were investigating mostly rodent and human eyes. Most scientists didn't even know about the existence of ocelli. I felt it was time to trade ignorance for knowledge and explore new territory.

I think Papa would have approved.

In 1985, the Russian scientist Stanislav (Slava) Tomarev inquired whether he could come to my laboratory for a year as a visiting scientist from the N. K. Koltzov Institute of Developmental Biology in Moscow. The cold war in the 1980s made it difficult to deal with the Soviet Union. I needed to make an appointment several days or weeks in advance with an international operator to speak to him (emails didn't exist yet), and often the call was scheduled in the middle of the night. It took four years to get Slava to NIH (where he remains, almost thirty years later). It was well worth the wait.

In Moscow, Slava had already started investigating the squid eye, which resembles a vertebrate eye with a large transparent lens. Squids are mollusks and, like octopus, are known as cephalopods. Slava continued his studies on the squid eye in my laboratory, which launched our research on invertebrate eyes. He found that the major crystallin of the squid and octopus lens was an entirely different enzyme-crystallin from those used in vertebrate lenses. In addition, unlike the enzyme-crystallin genes in vertebrates, the squid enzyme-crystallin gene had duplicated extensively, creating a large family of similar proteins.(34)

I also investigated the eye lens of scallops – also mollusks (bivalves) with hard shells like clams – which few people even knew had eyes. Scallops have as many as sixty sky-blue, lens-containing eyes spread evenly along the mantle, a tissue that lines the rims of the two shells. We showed that the scallop lens accumulates one of the minor enzyme-crystallins of the cephalopod lens, which is also found in the mammalian elephant shrew lens. The scallop enzyme-crystallin gene, like those of vertebrates, had not duplicated, as had the major cephalopod enzyme-crystallin gene.

Thus, cephalopods and scallops, despite their distant evolutionary history from vertebrates and their aquatic environment, had diverse enzyme-crystallins in their lens, extending the gene-sharing concept to invertebrate lenses.

A word about evolution: Eyes in widely different species such as squids or humans could look grossly similar either because they originated twice – once in the invertebrate lineage of squid and once in the vertebrate lineage of humans – and subsequently evolved independently to end points that appear grossly similar. This process is called convergent evolution. Alternatively, a primitive eye could have originated only once early in evolution and made differing modifications in different species during evolution. This could result in some eyes, like compound eyes of insects, appearing very different, but others, like squid and humans, looking grossly similar to each other. This process is called divergent evolution.

The question boiled down to how many times did an eye originate from scratch?

Historically, the squid eye was believed to resemble the vertebrate eye by convergent evolution. This would mean that squid and vertebrate eyes looked similar even though they originated separately and evolved independently. However, Walter Gehring from the University of Zurich questioned convergent evolution of eyes in invertebrates and vertebrates by providing experimental evidence based on development that all eyes – including invertebrate compound eyes and vertebrate camera-type eyes – evolved from one common ancestral eye, i.e., the eye originated only once. Slava and I teamed with Gehring to support (but not prove) the possibility that squid and vertebrate eyes looked similar due to divergent evolution. However, whether the squid and the vertebrate eye actually evolved from a common ancestor, and thereby were linked in evolution, or evolved separately by convergent evolution, remained inconclusive.*(35)*

The recurring mantra – the more we know, the more we need to learn – shouted in my mind with every new finding.

Crystallins were a jumble of entirely different properties, yet they all contributed to lens transparency and ability to focus an image on the retina. Moreover, crystallins had other functions – including heat protection and enzyme activities – unrelated to the optical properties of the lens. What molecular features, if any, might unify these diverse crystallins? The problem was as baffling as finding that a screwdriver, hammer and chisel could each turn a screw (which, of course, they can't), defying our common sense that similar tools are necessary for similar jobs. It was as radical a concept as Marcel Duchamp showing that a toilet can be art if it was put in a museum.

By extending our investigations to invertebrates, we unified the basketful of diverse crystallins by showing that similar (not identical) DNA sequence motifs were selected as control switches to "turn on" different crystallin genes in the lens, whether the gene resided in a mouse or a scallop. This indicated that upgrading the low expression of a gene encoding an enzyme in many tissues to high expression in the lens made the enzyme act as a lens crystallin. Thus, how the genes were controlled was a major contributing factor to having a protein selected as a lens crystallin. An apt analogy might be that the nature of a light switch influenced the color of the light bulb, a counter-intuitive idea. Thus, the diverse crystallins shared a common genetic "signature" via their regulatory mechanism for high lens expression.

The foray into cephalopods and scallops showed the value of comparative studies. But it was another creature that most captured my imagination.

At Masada in Israel, with Anton and Lona on my right
and Auran on my left, 2016.

The Wilderness of
Ignorance

I learned that jellyfish have ocelli (simple eyes) while browsing through a book on invertebrate vision. How could that be? Jellyfish – squishy globs that drifted in the sea using their tentacles, which were notorious for painful stings, to trap nutrients – seemed the least likely animal to have eyes. Also, jellyfish were one of the earliest multicellular species of animals to appear on Earth, estimated at 700-800 million years ago. It is not known if the jellyfish ocelli appeared that early in evolution or if they evolved later. Despite that I had studied eyes and lenses for approximately twenty years, I had no idea that jellyfish could see anything. I doubted whether any of my colleagues knew either, although the jellyfish ocelli had been discovered in the late 19th century.

The pictures of jellyfish ocelli showed resemblances to camera-type eyes of vertebrates – a reduced cornea comprising a single layer of cells in front of a bulging transparent lens, and black pigment behind the retina to protect against light scatter. There was no space between the lens and retina, unlike the situation in the eyes of squid, scallop and vertebrates, where the space (filled with transparent connective tissue called the vitreous) allowed incoming light to bend to a focal point on the retina to produce a clear image.*(36)* I love the idea that spacing between tissues requires as much evolutionary selection as the tissues themselves. It's as important and comparable to negative space in a sculpture, or to composition in a painting.

Were the jellyfish lens crystallins enzyme-crystallins? I was keen to jump into the universe of jellyfish, another step for me into marine biology: barnacles in college, sea urchins in graduate school, cephalopods and scallops, and now jellyfish. I saw a chance to write a new scientific chapter on lens and crystallins.

But, how to go about studying jellyfish eyes in my landlocked laboratory at NIH? There was no commercial source for jellyfish as there was for squid and scallops. The sea was the only source of jellyfish, and I had no idea how to get them there. Moreover, with small exceptions, the ocelli occurred only in specific species belonging to cubozoans (known as box jellyfish due to their symmetrical, box-like shape).

I found an article on a cubozoan jellyfish co-authored by Charles Cutress written ten years earlier at the marine laboratory in La Parguera, Puerto Rico, an affiliate of the University of Puerto Rico. I contacted Cutress and he responded saying that he would teach me how to capture *Tripedalia cystophora*, a jellyfish that has ocelli and resides in the mangrove swamp in La Parguera, and that he would let me work in his laboratory.

I called my colleague, Joseph Horwitz, a professor at the Jules Stein Eye Institute at UCLA School of Medicine with whom I'd collaborated for many years and asked him if he wanted to go on an adventure with me to study jellyfish vision.

"Are you kidding? Jellyfish have eyes?"

I wasn't kidding. Joe agreed, and off we went in search of a new world of research.

Upon landing in humid San Juan, we rented a car and drove to La Parguera, still just a name to us, exhilarated by a sense of freedom from obligations and bureaucracy. Research in the wild! We were on a great scientific adventure to discover crystallins in the jellyfish ocellus, which almost no one in the world knew existed.

The jellyfish we were after had four dangling structures (called rhopalia) in small notches equally spaced around the surface bell. Each rhopalium had one large ocellus facing upward and one small ocellus facing downward, as well as two simple eyespots (one round, the other just a slit), which comprised only photoreceptors, on each side of the two lens-containing ocelli. The eyespots detected light, but without lenses or any type of eye structure wouldn't be able to see an image. Jellyfish vision and light reception seemed even more complex than our own.

Due to the arrangement of the rhopalia, the jellyfish should see simultaneously in all directions – up, down and all around – a remarkable adaptation for their three-dimensional environment in water. In addition to ocelli, each rhopalium had an organ (called a statocyst) to sense up from down. Imagine, squeezing all that sensory complexity into rhopalia only about two hundredths of an inch in diameter. Jellyfish may have appeared early in evolution, but they were hardly primitive, a misconception by scientists and laymen alike. Jellyfish, among the first multicellular animals to appear on Earth, were highly adapted for their niche, and I was eager to learn their secrets.

As we drove, the difference between impulse and reality suddenly worried me. Would we be able to catch enough jellyfish for our experiments? I may have been an expert at dissecting tiny tissues due to the years I spent dissecting embryonic chicken lenses, but would I be able to surgically excise the minuscule ocelli from the jellyfish or their even more microscopic lenses? And so-what if, as likely, I found a strange crystallin no one has ever heard of in the jellyfish lens? Did I really want to jump into the murky puddle of jellyfish with no clear vision beyond adding the name of another protein to the list of crystallins? Was I willing to roll the dice on my career for jellyfish, especially in view of the shifting balance of government funding away from purely basic research in favor of medically-related research? As my thoughts vacillated, a quote from Einstein flashed through my mind: "If we knew what we were doing, it wouldn't be called research." If that was good enough for Einstein, it was good enough for me. But was it good enough for NIH?

Aware of the risks, I funded my jellyfish travels rather than use my NIH allowance. So, there I was, a government-employed lab chief on a private excursion to the mangrove swamps in Puerto Rico to study jellyfish ocelli, which had no direct medical relevance yet. But wasn't that true when starting any project in basic science research? Basic research was driven by curiosity, intuition and *potential* applications, which often never occur or take much time to materialize.

The next morning Joe and I took a ferry for a two-minute hop from the mainland to the marine station on a small island. When I stepped off the ferry, an iguana scampered across my path, and the more of the prehistoric creatures showed themselves. I took that as a positive omen to learn from the ancient jellyfish.

We found Charles (Chuck) Cutress in his office, and after some small talk, Chuck snatched several bottles of water, a few small dip-nets to capture the jellyfish, and took off, saying, "Let's go get 'em." We followed enthusiastically into a rowboat with an outboard motor and headed for the nearby mangrove swamp.

Chuck skillfully guided the boat along the edge of town. The wind swept my face, the sun warmed my body, and the gentle bounces of the boat against the choppy waves were comforting. I closed my eyes, appreciating the moment. It was that same sense of freedom I felt on the ferry to Millport in Scotland and, later, to Friday Harbor Laboratories in Puget Sound. It felt right.

Once in the swamp, Chuck headed the boat directly into the thick mass of trees and put the motor in neutral. Roots projected from the branches of the mangrove trees into the muddy bottom of the shallow water. Life teemed everywhere – crabs, sea anemones, tubeworms, small fish, algae, snails...and, oh my, mosquitoes. I became an appetizer for these voracious beasts.

Chuck spotted the small jellyfish by the boat. They swam by in jerky motions propelled by regular contractions of their translucent muscular surface bell by their tentacles reflecting the bright rays of sunlight that filtered through the leaves of the mangrove trees and penetrated the water with pencil-like tracks. He scooped them out of the water with the dip-net and dumped each into the bucket filled with seawater. Soon Joe and I were doing the same, but more slowly and with less skill. The largest jellyfish were only a fifth of an inch in diameter. Females were recognizable by their orange ovaries under the surface of the bell; inspection under the microscope later showed some females were filled with thousands of swarming orange embryos. Males had vertical white streaks of testes beneath the bell, which were easily seen.

I wondered whether the jellyfish had any destination in the lagoon, or whether they communicated with each other, since they often traveled in groups. I began to appreciate the strength and resilience of these ancient aquatic animals. They consumed small crustaceans and tiny fish that could be seen still undigested in their stomachs under the dissecting microscope back in the laboratory. They were vigorous little predators.

It was glorious collecting jellyfish in their lush, brackish environment and to feel a part, no matter how small, of the hugeness of nature.

When our buckets were packed with jellyfish, I didn't want to leave this secluded haven. I asked Chuck if we could take a quick look on the other side of the waterway for jellyfish.

"Never saw a jellyfish there," he said.

"How's that possible? Let's take a look," I said.

Joe nodded in agreement. Chuck agreed reluctantly.

We scanned the other side of the lagoon for jellyfish and didn't find any. We then went to another lagoon close by, and then another. Again: no jellyfish. Chuck was right. The jellyfish congregated only at the spot he had taken us to.

Strange, I thought: how come all the jellyfish congregate in only one spot?

Chuck told us about another species *(Carybdea marsupialis)* three or four times larger than the ones we'd caught in the mangrove swamp that also had well-developed eyes. They could be caught at night from the dock of the marine laboratory by shining an incandescent light on the surface of the water. After sunset, on our last night in La Parguera, we made our way down the sloping path from the laboratory to the dock hunting for *Carybdea*. The moonbeam split the bay in front of me in half; an iguana watched me from a few yards away; fireflies sparkled in the air; bioluminescence flashed on the surface of the bay. Jellyfish had already earned a special spot in me, despite that we had not discovered anything yet, and I feared maybe never would.

Joe plugged the lantern into an electric outlet on the dock and directed the light beam onto the water's surface. Dozens of small fish swarmed into the spotlight, and squid darted in and out of the bright patch with astounding speed, their arms giving the illusion of a rotating propeller. I had never seen a living thing move so fast. We waited for the jellyfish Chuck had promised us. Close to midnight we stared into our bucket containing nothing but water.

"Too bad," said Joe. He didn't sound as disappointed as I felt. He enjoyed the quiet evening in the moonlight.

"We tried," I responded. "At least we got lots of *Tripedalia* in the swamp the last couple of days."

As we were preparing to call it a night, I noticed an angelic white form with lace-like tentacles, a single jellyfish, rising in the water toward the light. I watched transfixed by its majesty. Why had it taken so long to arrive? Did it live directly below the dock or had it traveled from afar? How far? What did the jellyfish see and what would it do with the information? I dipped the net into the water and gently scooped it up as it was making a U-turn to head back down to deeper, safer water. I felt guilty ripping this adventuresome jellyfish, lured by the light, from his natural habitat. The jellyfish didn't deserve such a fate.

Five more jellyfish followed within as many minutes. We placed each one in the bucket.

As with *Tripedalia*, *Carybdea* seemed to travel in groups, or perhaps as a family of sorts. I wondered if and how they communicated with one another. No more jellyfish appeared during the next fifteen minutes. We took the six jellyfish we captured to the laboratory. The next morning, we excised and froze the rhopalia to take them back home to our laboratories for analysis.

In my laboratory at NIH I found that the jellyfish had three different crystallins, all new that had not yet been represented in the lenses of other species or even in the growing database of known proteins.(37) One of the three jellyfish crystallins showed a weak relationship to a metabolic enzyme implicated in stress protection and seemed to be present in jellyfish tissues outside of the lens. Another of the three jellyfish crystallins appeared related to a different metabolic enzyme, and it too appeared to be present in other tissues of the jellyfish. Thus, our analysis of jellyfish lens crystallins suggested that gene sharing started as an evolutionary strategy already in jellyfish, one of the first multicellular animals to appear on the planet.

Later, Zbynek Kozmik, a visiting scientist from the Czech Republic, and I provided evidence for structural and biochemical similarities between the jellyfish ocellus and the vertebrate eye.(38) Who would have imagined comparing human eyes with jellyfish ocelli? What if, I mused, future studies discovered a "magic" protein in the jellyfish ocellus that promoted regeneration of photoreceptors in human macular degeneration, a common blinding eye pathology? Why not? Jellyfish were the source of the green florescent protein (GFP) that revealed processes of gene expression, nerve cell development and metastasis of cancer cells that won the 2008 Nobel Prize in chemistry.

As gene sharing had brought attention to the lens, our research on invertebrates put a spotlight on jellyfish, and prompted other laboratories to investigate jellyfish vision. In particular, Dan Erik-Nilsson and his colleagues in Sweden showed that, even with almost no space between the lens and retina to generate a focal point as in vertebrate eyes, jellyfish should be able to see blurred images. Why the jellyfish would evolve blurred instead of focused vision is puzzling. I see this as another example of a "small problem" that is probably a "large problem" not yet solved.

One drawback of doing research on little-studied species is that even simple procedures can create frustrating, time-consuming obstacles. For example, extracting DNA from tissues was routine, less than a day's work. Yet in jellyfish, some sticky substance always created a gummy mess when extracting DNA using the protocol for extraction designed for vertebrates. I worked for months trying to extract pure jellyfish DNA, until I extracted it from isolated ovaries or testes of the jellyfish, which worked well, a suggestion in a publication by Eric Davidson at Caltech. Unexpected problems, often trivial, causing lost time are unavoidable when venturing to anything new.

When I started my research on jellyfish, I showed an electron micrograph of a histological section through the jellyfish lens to the NEI Scientific Director, Jin Kinoshita. I asked him if he could identify the image.

"I'm not sure, Joram," he said cautiously.

"Take a guess," I said.

"Well, it looks somewhat like a human lens," he responded.

"Close," I said. "It's a jellyfish lens."

"JELLYFISH!!"

"Yes," I answered softly. "Jellyfish."

That was one of my great satisfactions of basic research: exploring the unknown, being surprised. Much basic research is wandering in confusion, trying, hoping and identifying problems rather than solving them, at least at first.

I made a risky plug for basic research once by invoking jellyfish when the Board of Scientific Counselors (BSCs) – a panel of leading scientists outside of NIH – reviewed my laboratory, as occurred every four or five years. It went like this.

Carl Kupfer, the NEI Director, called me into his office to check on what I planned to present to the BSCs. "You realize, Joram," he said, "these reviews are in the public domain and affect all of us. Congress sees them as well."

Resentful, since I'd never been drilled before on my research presentations to the BSCs, I gave him a quick, but respectful, rundown of what I'd planned to speak about. I didn't mention jellyfish, which was a side project.

A few weeks later, I stood before the BSC reviewing panel and NEI staff, including Kupfer, in a windowless conference room filled to capacity. I devoted about twenty minutes of my allotted half hour to my research on the lens and cornea of the mouse eye. But jellyfish buzzed in my mind. I had prepared a power point slide of the jellyfish ocellus but had left it to impulse at the moment whether or not to show it. That moment arrived as I looked out at my captive audience.

"To conclude," I said, with a burst of self-confidence, "I would like to tell you about our studies on...," I hesitated, strategically, not for loss of words, "...the jellyfish eye." Saying eye had greater impact than ocellus. Words matter.

Kupfer, sitting in the front close to me, looked stunned. But the BSC panel members seemed curious, and that encouraged me.

"It is commonly believed," I went on, "that the eye is an outgrowth of the brain, making it a part of the central nervous system." That the retina belongs to the central nervous system was often stressed, using the importance of the brain as a magnet for funding vision research.

"Our preliminary work on the jellyfish suggests that the eye may not have originated as an outgrowth of the brain," I said.

Kupfer's face turned pastel green. The BSC members moved to the edge of their seats. I crossed my fingers and flashed a photomicrograph of a jellyfish ocellus on the screen, confident that no one in the audience had ever seen a picture of one and didn't know that jellyfish could see anything. Oh, what fun that was! And, how beautiful, how mysterious, how intoxicating that jellyfish eye was in all its glory, peering from the screen at the audience of confused experts on vision.

I had everyone's attention, especially Kupfer's.

"But, wait a minute, where's the brain?" I asked rhetorically. "There doesn't seem to be one."

I paused, and then pointed out that jellyfish occupied the base of the evolutionary tree and first appeared on Earth seven to eight hundred million years ago, in contrast to humans, who were relative newcomers on the planet. Yet, there it was: a small sophisticated jellyfish eye with a lens, a simplified cornea and a retina with photoreceptors buried in pigment, looking grossly like a human eye. The photo-receptors were even ciliated, like human photoreceptors, and unlike the photoreceptors in other invertebrates. Jellyfish were not globs of goo; they were complex organisms with ocelli that could be confused with vertebrate eyes at first glance, as Kinoshita did for the lens.

But, no brain, just some scattered ganglia and a nerve ring circling the jellyfish; there was nothing that resembled a brain, as we know it.

The audience stirred.

I continued. "Wouldn't any species that had such highly developed eyes need to evolve some kind of brain to interpret whatever it sees? Images, or any form of light detection, must serve some purpose, although we don't know what that is yet for jellyfish. That's why I wonder if the brain, the seat of thought, is an evolutionary outgrowth of the eye, not the other way around, as everyone takes for granted. Eyes first, in jellyfish, then brains later."

There was a moment of silence as the review panel digested the idea of jellyfish eyes preceding brains. I had turned the conventional order of the eye as an out-pouching of the brain upside down. I thought of Papa, who often flipped ideas, took people by surprise, like "the speed of dark."

Standing before world experts on the eye, I realized that Papa's fanciful dreams of a scientist's life were metaphors for a utopia devoid of the hardships and anguish he had endured and the loneliness of a musician's life traveling the globe away from his family, even though he sat on a throne of success. The jellyfish ocellus represented my life in science, not a metaphor. The ocellus was a gem of evolution that extended my research on lens crystallins and gene sharing. I suddenly saw fact intertwined with imagination, each enriched by the other, and I felt challenged more than ever to tease the truth out of jellyfish and the other species and ideas that filled my life.

The gray, government conference room became a fantasyland, but also as real as the ground I walked on. I knew that I was speculating and creating an interesting narrative from little information that could be interpreted in various ways. But I also knew that I was confronting challenging questions – important questions – searching for new ideas, as if testing different pieces of a puzzle to form an image. I wasn't afraid to make a mistake, because without mistakes there would be no progress, as I'd implied to Kupfer when I established my laboratory, in the same way that without mutations there would be no evolution. That was basic science as I imagined it, as I wanted it to be – mysterious, riveting and alluring – an adventure in the wilderness of ignorance.

When I concluded my talk, David Hubel, a member of the reviewing panel, exclaimed, "Imagine! A jellyfish eye! Who would have thought? If I hadn't been allowed to follow my nose, I never would have won the Nobel Prize."

Sweet words! But did the same sentiment apply to those who will not win a Nobel Prize?

In La Parguera, Puerto Rico dissecting jellyfish eyes, 1985.

Multiple Perspectives

When I gave the 2002 Russell Marker Lectures at Pennsylvania State University, Alan Walker, a professor at the university, suggested that I write a book on gene sharing. When I returned to my laboratory at NIH a few days later, he had already contacted Michael Fisher, an editor at Harvard University Press. Fisher came to NIH to see me and seemed receptive for me to write a book on gene sharing. Although I was excited about the prospect and happy that Harvard thought it worthwhile, I suddenly had cold feet about committing to a book. My concern was whether gene sharing applied only to lens crystallins or whether it was a more pervasive phenomenon. Did other proteins have multiple functions? If not, would a book on lens crystallins alone be any more worthwhile than the several extensive reviews I'd written already on the subject?

Before accepting to write a book, I started reading articles to determine how many proteins might be specialized for more than one function. I hoped to find at least a small handful that performed two or more entirely different tasks. By different tasks, I meant as different as a thimble or a brick. For example, bricks can be used to construct a house or a fence. While these are different structures, they both use bricks as a building material. An analogy to gene sharing would be using a brick as part of a house, or as an object to paint for creating art. The house/art difference is analogous to crystallins being used as a structural component in the lens or as a metabolic enzyme in numerous tissues. I hoped to find a few proteins with compelling evidence for gene sharing, or at least with believable evidence suggesting gene sharing.

Much to my surprise, gene sharing seemed common among the proteins I read about – metabolic enzymes, hemoglobin, membrane surface proteins, and a host of others. Many proteins had at least two separate functions and some five or six, depending on the tissue they inhabited and the physiological conditions.

Feeling confident that gene sharing was not limited to lens crystallins, I signed a contract and wrote *Gene Sharing and Evolution.(39)* Writing the book allowed me to consider the relevance of gene sharing beyond protein function *per se*, such as the elusive concept of the gene, or the role of networks regulating biological processes, or estimating the number of genes. The number of human genes has been estimated in the neighborhood of 22,000. But, if a gene encoded a protein with several different functions, should it be considered as one or several genes? Genes were often named by the function of the protein they encoded, or even by the absence of its normal function if mutated or deleted. For example, "eyeless" is an example of a gene that, when mutated, resulted in a fly without eyes. However, the "eyeless" protein (known as pax6 in science jargon) turned out to be a factor that regulated many different genes during development. What, then, to name, or how to count, a gene that encodes a protein with multiple functions, as the crystallin genes do in gene sharing?

I concluded that gene sharing was a pragmatic process in the sense that genes and proteins were promiscuous, doing whatever was possible under different circumstances without relinquishing their other roles. Proteins weren't designed for a single purpose; they added new functions when conditions changed (different cellular environment; expressed at different concentrations) or when present in different tissues. Gene sharing was an example of serendipity followed by natural selection if their new function was beneficial, or at least not detrimental. I proposed in the preface of the book that "...distinct specialized functions required for life are carried out by the same proteins cast as different characters, much as in a Peter Sellers movie."

Two reasons stand out that make gene sharing surprising and novel. First, gene sharing cautions us about being overly confident we understand the nature of any protein by its name or one of its known functions. This leaves open that we've missed something important that might give us an alternative, or deeper, understanding of what we thought we knew.

Consider the following analogy with gene sharing that I experienced as a boy.

Our school principal died unexpectedly of a heart attack when I was in the eighth grade. I was shocked, as were the other students. When I read his obituary a few weeks later, I was taken by surprise to discover that he acted as one of the clowns in the Ice Capades every time they came to town. I must have seen him streaming out of a packed car on the ice with other clowns or zigzagging on his skates pretending to be drunk while chased by another skater masquerading as a monster, but I had no idea that the clown was my very own school principal.

The individual who died had the label of "principal," not "clown," so it surprised me – enlarged my view of him – to discover that he was both. He changed from a principal to a principal/clown. School and the Ice Capades had nothing in common, until linked by my school's principal's hidden life, a human analogy to gene sharing.

We are accustomed to using different files to create order. Labels influence how we think about whatever has been named. Michael Lewis describes in *The Undoing Project* how the nickname "Man Boobs" blocked the recruitment of a talented basketball player (who later became a star) by a professional team. What's in a name? Confirmation bias, Lewis called it: we are blinded by the name, which causes us to miss buried traits.*(40)*

Gene sharing also negates our deep-seated notion that specialization and diversification are polar opposites. We assume that being highly specialized for one function is at odds with also being equally specialized for a completely different function. As I'd mentioned above, we never consider the same person to be highly specialized for multiple roles – a jack-of-all-trades. We don't go to a lawyer to treat a medical problem, or to a car mechanic when we need an architect. Specialization and diversification lie at opposite ends of the spectrum in our minds. Gene sharing shatters that myth for proteins. A single gene and its encoded protein can specialize over millions of years for several entirely different functions, each highly specialized.

Gene sharing proves that specialization and diversification can go hand-in-hand without having one job interfere with the other. I called the paradox of specialization with diversification "a specialist's nightmare" in *Gene Sharing and Evolution.*

Writing the book gave me a chance to speculate on numerous implications of gene sharing in medicine and in the pharmaceutical industry. I quote from the end of *Gene Sharing and Evolution:*

"We may anticipate that the concept of gene sharing will become increasingly important in this scientific world of multifunctional proteins, interactive pathways, and genomic medicine. Finally, the modular nature of proteins, like the modular nature of all biological organizations, suggests that it will be possible to engineer proteins to assume new, potentially therapeutic functions without deleterious effects on their normal function – in essence, to create new roles for endogenous polypeptides to treat and/or prevent diseases.

"Overall, the paradox of gene sharing – that proteins specialize and diversify simultaneously – opens countless possibilities and lays as many minefields. The trick is to observe Nature without bias and appreciate its resourcefulness, think imaginatively, dare to take a chance, and expect the unexpected."

I was gratified to receive the 2008 Helen Keller Prize for Vision Research, which portrayed gene sharing as an example of how strictly basic research could blend into practical applications. I gave one example in my acceptance remarks. "The recognition that crystallins, as well as many other proteins, are multifunctional proteins expressed in many tissues provides possible connections to explore between apparently unrelated diseases. An example of linked disease is cataract developing in association with myopathies due to mutation of the small heat shock protein, αB-crystallin, which is also a heat shock protein. Understanding connections between apparently unrelated disorders might facilitate early diagnoses and relieve multiple symptoms by appropriate treatment."

I gave many other examples on the potential medical relevance of gene sharing, including caution in the use of animal models for investigations of human disease. For example, different species sometimes use different proteins to perform the same function. Gene sharing is also relevant for drug development by targeting the intended function of multifunctional proteins.

I ended my talk saying, "By recognizing basic research in contrast to goal oriented translational research that is emphasized so much today, I believe that you make an invaluable and timely contribution to science in general and hasten the eventual conquest of blindness and other devastating disorders."

The point is that a single perspective is never sufficient. A beautifully constructed sentence carries more weight than the words alone convey; music can tempt peace in the despair of war; Mona Lisa transcends the name of Leonardo da Vinci's subject.

Science, too, is more than dispassionate laws of nature: it's a human perspective of nature, and it's often driven by passion, like art.

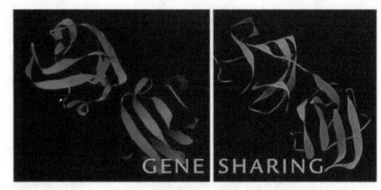

GENE SHARING

AND EVOLUTION

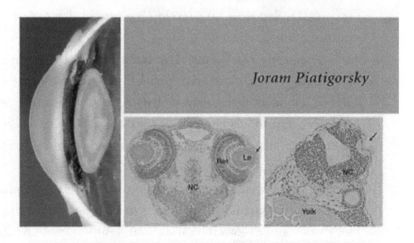

Joram Piatigorsky

THE DIVERSITY OF PROTEIN FUNCTIONS

Gene Sharing and Evolution book cover.

Riding the Goat

When I gave the keynote lecture at the first NEI symposium, Focus on Fellows, in 2007, I stressed the importance of basic research in my career, but was at loss to answer a postdoctoral fellow who asked me afterwards what I thought he should work on.

"I don't know," I said. "What interests you?"

What could I say? Predict the future of science, which depends on discoveries not made yet? It was like a waiter at a restaurant, when asked what's best on the menu, saying that it depends on what you like. Really?

Although scientific research analyzes external nature, I have always felt a strong internal component to my research – a personal odyssey that reflected my background and previous experiences. My career in science was greatly influenced by my family of artists, and by being financially secure, self-directed and eager to make a mark. How could I advise the postdoctoral fellow what he should choose as a research project? I knew nothing about him. While scientists all study nature in one form or other, constantly changing technical and conceptual considerations affect what is possible to understand at any one time. Perhaps next year, projects that are pipedreams today will become possible or even routine. Also, scientists are sufficiently different that no two careers will follow the same trajectory. The Australian Nobel laureate, Peter Medawar, stated this emphatically in his book, *Advice to a Young Scientist*: "There is no such person as the scientist…they are a collection as various in temperament as physicians, lawyers, clergymen, attorneys, or swimming-pool attendants." *(41)*

I valued originality and always leaned towards the academic Ivory Tower. However, I always kept in mind the distinction between new knowledge and new concepts. I expressed my preference for the latter in a commentary in the NIH publication, *Catalyst,* where I vented my frustration with the growing pressures to justify research on the basis of medical relevance.*(42)* My commentary – metaphorical fiction – started with a young boy who wanted to sit on a metal goat statue and imagine his future, as I had sat on such a goat in Rittenhouse Square in Philadelphia when I was a kid:

"Why are you crying, son?" asked the gray-haired gentleman when he came upon a little boy in Philadelphia's Rittenhouse Square. It was mid-April, flowers all abloom, weather perfect. The young boy was no more than five years old. He looked pitiful, with large dewdrops dripping from both eyes and his nose sniffling. His T-shirt was ripped under the left arm and he was sitting alone on the edge of the wooden bench. The boy looked up at the gentleman.

"Where's your mommy or daddy?"

"Dunno. My mommy told me to wait here."

"Don't be scared. I'm sure she will return in just a few minutes. Where did she go?"

"I'm not scared." And then he started crying again.

"So why are you crying? What's so sad?"

More sniffles. Then the boy said, "My mommy never lets me climb on the goat statue. That's what I want to do."

"Why not?" asked the gentleman.

"She says that I could fall off and get hurt. She says that kids aren't supposed to climb on it and if I do the other kids will also want to. So what?"

"What does she want you to do at the park?" asked the gentleman, becoming interested.

"I dunno. She wants me to play with the other kids."

"Don't you want to do that? I see a lot of kids about your age running around."

"No. I want to climb on top of the goat."

"What would you do there, on top of the goat?"

Long pause. The tears were gone now, and the little boy's eyes had a mischievous gleam.

"I'd sit there and look around and pretend I was exploring. I did it once when my mommy wasn't watching. Everything looked different up there. I could see across the street, and the birds seemed closer. It was exciting. I dreamed that..."

"Yes, go on. What did you dream of?"

The boy's head drooped and then he whispered, "I'm not supposed to talk to strangers. There's my mommy coming."

The gentleman stepped aside and watched as the little boy slid off the park bench and walked sullenly away beside his mother. They passed directly in front of the goat, but the boy's stare never budged from the pavement as they disappeared into the distance.

The postdoctoral fellows who were at my lecture might have felt like the little boy wanting to ride the goat. When I started my career, I assumed that inspiring daydreams and playful exploration were critical components of creative research. Indeed, the Nobel Laureate François Jacob advanced the idea that innovation and evolution depended on tinkering – trial and error by random mutations. I would be hard-pressed to argue that what works for innovation in nature doesn't for advances in science.

I rode the metaphorical goat throughout my years in science rather than follow someone else's agenda.

I remember my irritation at a meeting of laboratory chiefs when the NEI Director suggested that all the postdoctoral fellows should spend time in the clinic exposed to patients. "This would change the direction of research of all the fellows no matter what they thought when they came here," he said. "They must see for themselves the problems of these afflictions."

I understood. Words can't compete with tears; seeing a tornado on screen paled next to having withstood one. I wondered, however, why change the direction of an enthusiastic postdoctoral fellow pursuing basic research? What about those who favored basic exploratory research – those who wanted to ride the goat? What about Charles Darwin, who quit medical school after attending clinics and witnessing surgery, especially on children without anesthesia, in order to pursue his revolutionary studies on evolution?

Nods went around the table supporting the suggestion that all postdoctoral scientists be exposed to patients with eye ailments. One laboratory chief said that his goals were reset after he had spent time in the clinic.

More nods.

Beginning to stew, I blurted out, "But not everyone wants to be or should be a physician. Some are driven by other considerations and talents."

The group was quiet.

I continued. "I'm sure that it would benefit some individuals to spend time in the clinic, but why everyone? Why not make it an option?"

Everyone sat silently, waiting for me to put my foot deeper into my mouth, perhaps to swallow it altogether!

"I believe we should provide an environment where each person can cultivate his or her own passion and have opportunities to develop their research direction, all within appropriate boundaries. Preferences and talents differ. I favor exploiting those preferences."

There. I'd expressed my views.

Mandatory time in the clinic for all postdoctoral fellows never happened during my tenure at the NEI.

I never wavered in my devotion to basic science. As one of the first NEI panel members establishing priorities for cataract research from 1980 to 1985, I influenced switching the first priority from research on the human lens with a cataract to research on the normal, healthy lens, regardless of species. My argument was that defining normal – healthy –

provided the parameters to determine abnormal – ill. There's enough on "normal" to fill a lifetime of research for those who are so inclined. Priority number one for the national plan for cataract research list became "The Normal Lens."

My first priority for any research was always rigorous and disciplined research by scientists with an open mind. Let the chips fall where they may, and that was often in unexpected places with surprising rewards.

In a discussion with the scientific director of the National Eye Institute many years ago, I brought up the research topics presented at the recent meeting of the Association for Research in Vision and Ophthalmology (ARVO), the largest basic science eye meeting. At my last count there had been about a dozen scattered research reports on invertebrate eyes, except for the popular compound eye of the fruit fly *Drosophila,* among the approximate ten thousand reports on vertebrate eyes (principally human and rodent eyes).

"Since relatively little is known about invertebrate eyes, wouldn't it be smart to develop a section at the NEI to study them?" I suggested. "They are more diverse and numerous than vertebrate eyes and different enough to teach us a lot about vision and eyes that we don't know. So many research findings would be new. A small investment could become a major source of discoveries in vision science."

As I spoke I imagined novel concepts bursting forth from experiments on the visual systems of spiders and copepods and snails.

"Even some protozoans have specialized eye organelles, which are subcellular structures that have a lens and retina of sorts," I said, hoping to kindle his curiosity.

My mind was racing with questions that I would have loved to explore. Why did a single cell need vision? What did they see? What did they do with the visual information? How did they transform light into behavior? Did light attract or repel them? What happened if the protozoan becomes blind? After all, most protozoans didn't have eye organelles and they seemed to do just fine. Research in that esoteric area had no alternative but adding to our knowledge of vision, since so little was known about eye organelles, or invertebrate ocelli for that matter.

The Scientific Director looked bored. "I'm not afraid of the competition," he said.

Competition? What competition? Then I realized he meant that he was wary about venturing beyond rodents and humans. He was ready and eager to continue focusing on eye pathologies affecting humans, but he wanted to do it faster and better than others exploring the same or similar problems. It was a race – a competition – with an artificial finish line.

Choosing competition over exploration seemed to be missing the point of science and relinquishing an opportunity for important discoveries.

What about the goat?

While I hesitated to advise the postdoctoral fellow who asked me for advice on what he should work on, today I would say that "following his nose," as Hubel expressed, was probably worth the risk, but also to remember Rall's warning that "not everything works." However, there is a growing requirement for grant requests to provide preliminary evidence that the proposed research will give the expected results. Isn't that contrary to the purpose and spirit of basic science? It discourages risk and minimizes the most exciting development of basic research: results that are not what were expected. The competition for funds, however, is real and must be respected. But beware of Catch 22: it isn't possible to know whether a project is worth doing until the results are known, a conflict worth considering while on the goat.

On occasion postdoctoral fellows have come to me despondent when their experiments didn't work. The problem is often defining "work." The expected result may not be the proper result. The experiment may well have worked, if the phenomena being investigated were understood.

"What to do next," they asked?

At first, I sympathized – I too wanted to see light at the end of the tunnel and often felt despondent with failures, but then I congratulated them for becoming scientists at the most challenging level.

"You are now in a position," I said, "to make a discovery, rather than parrot what you thought you already knew."

I could have invoked Einstein's view that research means not knowing what you're doing.

Certainly, science builds on incremental additions to a growing structure of knowledge. Isn't that true in all fields? But as the years went by, I watched, sometimes with dismay, as advances in technology shifted basic research towards commercialization and goal-oriented projects. The banter of daily conversation became less driven by curiosity than when the nature of genes and their expression defined the outer edge of research. That era too, as today's, was pregnant with promises for a golden future. And that bright future arrived – the era of recombinant DNA and molecular genetics – largely by unpredictable findings of basic research, such as the discoveries of heat-stable enzymes in microorganisms that live next to thermal vents deep in the ocean, and of bacterial enzymes (restriction enzymes) that cut DNA at specific sequences to protect themselves against viral infection. Sea changes, such as the discovery of antibiotics, were seldom the result of goal-oriented medical or industrial research.

At the risk of sounding pretentious, I considered myself an explorer in the whirlwind of baffling mysteries of nature. The least expected findings – gene sharing, for example – were my greatest rewards.

When on the metaphorical goat, I never knew if I sat high enough or saw far enough. I often felt some visions were mirages, as they probably were. At times I worried that I was resented for being too independent or privileged or selfish, such as going off to the mangrove swamps of Puerto Rico to track down jellyfish because I wanted to or could afford to do so. Sometimes I felt ridiculed as eccentric or unrealistic, as I sat on the metaphorical goat. However, optimism helped some of those dreams come true, for example, wanting to identify on-off switches of a gene before the new techniques in molecular genetics made it possible to do so. Perhaps my wildest dreams never became true, maybe because they lacked clarity or were too far astray from what I could do. I daydreamed about discovering phenomena in which energy considerations or wave properties led to yet unknown functions of the individual nucleotides of DNA beyond the genetic code itself, but I didn't know enough physics to even know if such questions made sense.

But I never felt that riding the goat and dreaming wasted my time. Those journeys in my mind became motivations and resulted in satisfactions and accomplishment in my career. Examples abound: I struggled to apply molecular analyses to tiny bits of cultured epithelia of embryonic chicken lenses, which required acrobatic skills of micro-dissection, before the recombinant DNA revolution made it possible. This skill did lead to some discoveries and became invaluable years later for dissecting scallop and jellyfish eyes. I investigated and lectured on chicken delta-crystallin to sparse audiences that could care less about this obscure crystallin, until its gene was cloned, and it earned a spot on the stage. I dove into the morass of crystallins in invertebrates that science had passed by, such as those in scallops and jellyfish at a time when no one was holding their breath for the results of my research. When others considered the transparent cornea and lens separately (the lens and cornea researchers hardly knew each other), I linked them together under the umbrella of crystallins in what I called the "refracton hypothesis," bringing attention to crystallins and gene sharing in the cornea.*(43)* I spent more time trying to open doors than closing them, sitting on that goat.

I tried my best to be who I was. Not everyone wants to ride the goat, not everyone should. It's not necessary to do so, but I did and have no regrets.

My family in front of Château de Ferrières at my uncle Guy's 90th birthday. From left to right: Auran (my older son), Joan Drachman (Evan's wife), Jephta, Mama, Evan (my nephew), Tonje Vetleseter (Auran's wife), Eric Drachman (my nephew), Anton (my younger son), Ava Roth (Anton's wife), Lona and me, 1999.

Under the Radar

Many activities occur under the radar in the life of a scientist, which I call my hidden life in science. These included reviewing manuscripts and grants and serving on editorial boards of professional journals and advisory panels. I have always benefitted from serving on committees and panels of various types. One regret, however, was rejecting an offer to serve on the NIH cell biology study section to review grants. In my mid-thirties I had participated on this study section on an ad hoc basis and found it enormously time-consuming. Accepting the offer meant reviewing dozens of grants three times a year for four years. I guarded my research time jealously. I believe it was very unusual for anyone to decline because it was an honor, apart from a learning experience and an important task to determine which grants to support.

One project I conceived had a significant impact. I organized a National Eye Institute – UCLA Conference on the molecular biology of the eye in Santa Fe in 1988 and edited the resulting book with Toshimichi Shinohara and Peggy Zelenka, section heads in my laboratory.*(44)* This international conference brought together, for the first time under the umbrella of molecular genetics, studies in diverse areas of the eye (photo transduction and retina, lens, and eye diseases: cancer, retinal degenerations, cataract, viral infections and connective disorders) and stimulated others with a similar approach, advancing the eye for basic studies.

Teaching at NIH was another activity under the radar. For many years, I taught a graduate level course in developmental biology, sometimes by myself and sometimes with invited colleagues, at the Foundation for Advanced Education in the Sciences, Inc., a private educational foundation at NIH. I also served as Chairman of the Department of Biology and Genetics from 1974-1987, and on the board of the foundation. One of the most positive aspects of teaching was my realization that much of my research related more to evolution than to developmental biology. What a surprise to learn about my own research on lens crystallins by teaching students, rather than by doing the work itself! Research can act as a funnel in which one swirls into deeper and narrower layers losing perspective without realizing it.

Although NIH did not grant academic degrees, I mentored a number of students from the United States and abroad who did their graduate research and wrote their PhD thesis in my laboratory, and postdoctoral fellows played the major role in my journey in science. If I had a mentorship style, it was to consider everyone individually, and to recognize that I had as much to learn from them as they had from me. Some would benefit by more frequent interactions with me, and others by less, and I tried to respect that.

Over the years I mentored forty or so postdoctoral scientists and was proud when they obtained high positions in academia and industry. Many became leaders in vision research. I was flattered when I was told that, at a conference in Hawaii on cataracts that I didn't attend, a group gathered informally to discuss what it was about my laboratory that generated successful scientific careers. I like to think that the answer was a stimulating environment that allowed each person to think independently and creatively. For example, one postdoctoral fellow from Europe asked me when starting his fellowship what his project would be.

"What do you mean?" I asked.

"What should I work on? Do you have a protocol for me?" He was anxious to get started.

A protocol? I'd never been asked that before. I had never given a postdoctoral fellow a precise research assignment, and certainly never a protocol to follow. At most, I'd suggested general topics that related to our ongoing studies.

"Well, what interests you?" I asked. "Any ideas?"

He looked unprepared for my question. I reviewed the projects in the laboratory, told him who was doing what, suggested some articles to read, and said we'd get together again after he had some time to think about possibilities for projects. I wanted to advance our studies on gene expression in the lens and suggested what I thought might be interesting and approachable areas of investigation. But I left the door open, believing that he would be more motivated and excited by his own ideas than mine.

Research may be posing external questions about nature, but it's driven largely by personal interest and ambition. Since choosing a specific research topic is one of the most important and difficult tasks of a basic scientist, I believe it should be part of postdoctoral training, even if

244

premature at the beginning stages of a science career. I had that opportunity when I was a postdoctoral fellow with Coulombre. Also, selfishly, I wanted to benefit from the thoughts and intuitions of bright postdoctoral fellows, as I hoped they would benefit from me and the other postdoctoral fellows in the laboratory. We all had the same challenges – trying to be creative and advancing science. The only difference between us was age and experience. Sometimes naïve eyes see more clearly than biased eyes. We educated and helped each other in whatever way we could.

In the early days when I had few postdoctoral fellows, they came to my home in Bethesda in the summer for a swim in the pool and a picnic lunch every Wednesday. We talked about family, future goals and science as well as other interests, and they got to know Lona and our two young boys. I continued contact with these postdoctoral fellows, although far too little, when they left to form their own careers. Our summer swims continued for a few years but stopped when the laboratory grew larger and the postdoctoral fellows multiplied. The result was that I had less opportunity to develop personal friendships with the members of the laboratory, which I regretted then and now. Sometimes smaller is better.

The most gratifying aspects of participating on scientific advisory panels and trustee boards were when I could be helpful, which occurred when I was a member of the Advisory Panel (1988-1992) and then the Board of Trustees (1993-1998) at the Whitney Laboratory for Marine Bioscience in St. Augustine Florida, an adjunct of the University of Florida located in Gainesville. Once a year, administrative members at the main campus reviewed the Whitney Laboratory and considered their requests for support. Although the support was deserved and received, I felt that it promoted a sense of dependency by the Whitney Laboratory on the parent university. Why not, I thought, reverse the process and have the Whitney give support to the parent university? To this end, I started an annual endowed lectureship – the Whitney Lecture. The chosen scientist, a major figure in the field selected by the Whitney Laboratory, would give the lecture at the main campus in Gainesville. The next day, he or she would visit the Whitney Laboratory, give an informal seminar and meet with the scientists. A few years after the lectureship was established, I received a call from the director of the Whitney saying that the university wanted to take control. I strongly urged him not to allow that to happen (I was no longer on the board). In my opinion this event had to remain a Whitney Laboratory contribution, and it has since its inception. The Whitney Lecturers have been Nobel Prize winners and other eminent scientists.

Many other activities in science were meaningful to me.

There were special lectures I gave that remain etched in my mind. The 1986 Friedenwald Award Lecture for the Association for Research in Vision and Ophthalmology attracted the largest audience I ever had, filling the Van Wezel auditorium in Sarasota, Florida. *(45)* That was my first attempt to project parallel power point slides on adjacent screens. All went well until the two projectors somehow went out of sync, partly because the podium was at the corner of the stage, making the screens hard for me to see, and partly my inexperience using two projectors simultaneously. I momentarily panicked and started moving the slides backwards and forwards on each projector. By a miracle, the two projectors synchronized again, but certainly not by anything I did consciously, and all went well.

And then there was the time that I was invited unexpectedly to visit a laboratory in Kyoto, Japan when I was attending the International Congress for Eye Research. When I arrived in Kyoto, I was taken to a room filled with scientists in a conference room. All eyes were focused on me.

Dr. Tokindo Okada, one of the central figures of developmental biology in Japan, turned to me.

"Dr. Piatigorsky, could you please give us a seminar on your research?"

I was totally unprepared and had no slides with me. I walked slowly to the front of the room, picked up a piece of chalk by the blackboard and forced myself to organize pronto. I wrote at the top of the right corner of the board, "Goals," and then walked slowly (to give myself time to think) across to the left corner of the board and wrote, "Question." The lecture was launched.

I started with a question we were trying to answer at the time, and sketched diagrams and graphs on the blackboard as I made my way across, until I reached "Goals." I ended with what we needed to do to achieve them. Despite the many lectures I gave nationally and internationally, all prepared, that impromptu lecture was one that especially satisfied me. It was born of necessity and worked. I couldn't repeat it. I don't have notes that I followed. As far as a lecture can be considered art, this was performance art, spontaneous and transient. I have often wondered how much we lose by analyzing and preparing too much.

Then there was the time I gave the Robert Kohn Lecture at Case Western Reserve University School of Medicine, for which I had prepared in-depth. However, a recent Nobel Laureate gave a lecture the hour before me in another part of the building, resulting in pitifully few people attending my talk. I gave the lecture, all went well, but my sense of failure ruled the day.

Hierarchy and recognition loom over research scientists, or at least I felt it so: awards, elections to prestigious societies, publications in journals with the highest impact factors, invitations to give named lectures or chair symposia at conferences. The trick is to keep perspective, and mainly, keep working. I confess, the question that has plagued me my entire career is, "When is enough?"

Perhaps never.

My hidden life under the radar at NIH also had its share of absurdities. Consider my discussion with the fire marshal. My laboratory was so overcrowded that once I threatened to put a stoplight at a junction between work-benches. The hallway, lined with centrifuges, refrigerators and freezers, was no better. One day I ran into the fire marshal in the hallway outside my crowded laboratory.

"Are you in charge here?" he asked with a frown.

I nodded.

"Well, doc, all this equipment can't stay in the hall. What if there's a fire?"

Although I knew we had more equipment in the hall than regulations permitted, there was no other place for us to put it, and we needed the equipment. I had no idea what to say: he was right, although other laboratories had the same problem. I had just finished reading *You Can Negotiate Anything* and thought that I might test negotiation techniques mentioned in the book. *(46)*

"I understand, marshal," I said. "A clogged hallway would hinder escape in case of a fire. That would be dangerous."

Now he knew that I knew his predicament and I wasn't just responding defensively. I continued, letting him know my problem.

"But we're so crowded here. I don't know what to do with all this stuff. Get rid of it? I could, I guess. But we need it for our work. Let me show you our predicament."

I wanted to show him what I was up against, so maybe he would empathize.

The marshal followed me into the lab. "I see what you mean, doc. Not much free space left."

"None," I said.

So far, so good.

"What do you recommend?" I asked.

Now he had to answer me, rather than vice-versa.

"I don't know," he admitted. "It's crowded, that's for sure."

"Wait, I have an idea," I said.

I took him into my cramped office, which was no more than a sliver of space carved out of the lab module. "What if I removed my desk and stuff equipment in here?"

I worried I was going overboard.

"But you need your desk, doc."

"Well...yes, true."

I hoped that he would consider us as two people with the same problem. We needed to clear the hall to satisfy him, but there was no available space to put the equipment, and I needed my desk as well as space to put the equipment.

"Tell me," I asked, "are the dimensions for free hall space written somewhere so I can try to follow them?"

"We're rewriting the specifications now, doc."

"It's in flux at the moment?"

"Yeah, I suppose so."

"Could you send me the new regulations when they're done, and I'll see what I can do?"

"No problem, doc. I'll do that. Thanks."

"Thank you," I responded.

I never heard from him again. Fortunately, we never had a fire.

And then there was the time when I met with the Animal Care and Use Committee at NIH. I'm strongly in favor of animal rights, however, the cumbersome forms, protocols and bureaucracy were problematic. For example, there was the time when I began to work on scallop eyes. I bought several dozen live scallops from the Marine Biological Laboratories at Woods Hole every few weeks and surgically removed their eyes lining the mantle.

"What are you doing to eliminate pain?" asked a committee member.

"Scallop pain?" I asked.

"Are you anesthetizing the scallops?"

I told the committee I had never seen an article on anesthetizing scallops, and that to the best of my knowledge most invertebrates died when treated with chemicals. I had no idea how to anesthetize scallops. It was hard enough just to keep them alive in captivity.

"I don't want to hurt any animal, but I don't think that the information is available concerning pain in scallops, or in any invertebrate for that matter," I said.

The committee members were not impressed.

I never heard from the committee about scallops again, and I continued my experiments.

But I still think about whether or not I hurt those animals.

There was a much earlier, more serious experience I had concerning conflict about animal rights. Many years ago, I was at dinner with Lona and guests. The Holocaust came up in the course of our conversation and, naturally, we all agreed that the Nazi atrocities were immoral beyond belief.

Suddenly I said, "What impresses me is that I believe everyone is susceptible to being immoral, and even killing, under certain conditions." I was thinking about a personal experience, not Hannah Arendt's banality of evil.

I received unflattering glances, but one gentleman looked incensed.

"I would *never* do such a thing," he said.

"But what if you had been indoctrinated to think in a certain way, were raised in such a culture, and were given orders to kill by your superiors?"

"Impossible! I would *never* carry out such orders." He was outraged. He was a good man, a kind man, and sincerely meant what he said.

Perhaps foolishly, I continued. "But what if your own life was at risk if you didn't follow orders, and if there were advantages – promotion, acceptance, praise – to join your peers and do what was expected? Your orders were more than military commands; they had become accepted customs. No one lives in social isolation." Then I added, "We no doubt harm people today ourselves if only by neglect."

I didn't mean to condone killing and cruelty. I was raising a discussion question. He wouldn't budge, and a chill was in the air.

So, I confessed what was really bothering me.

"Well," I said, "I'm doing research on protein synthesis and for that I need to grow a large batch of cancer cells – they're called Ascites cells – for my experiments."

My research career was in the early stages at NIH.

"So what?" he asked.

The others at the dinner table were intrigued.

"Well," I continued, "I grow the cancer cells in the abdomen of mice, then kill the mice and extract the cells. My problem is killing the mice."

"How do you do that?" he asked, now more interested than defensive.

"It's pretty bad," I said, and then I hesitated.

He waited for me to continue.

"I'm told that asphyxiation or poisons might harm the cells, and besides, those result in slow deaths. So, I place each mouse on the tabletop and quickly break its neck by yanking the tail with one hand while holding the head in place with the thumb of my other hand. Apparently, it's an immediate, painless death for the mouse, which seems correct, or at least I choose to believe that it is."

I heard a few, "Oh," and "That's awful." I was afraid that I looked like a monster and lost some friends. Still, I went on.

"But here's my problem," I said. "The first time I did this, I was horrified, felt nauseous, and wasn't even sure I could continue to kill the mice. I did nonetheless, because I had to if I was going to continue my experiments. I justified the killings as necessary sacrifices for medical advancement."

I also knew (as no doubt did my guests) that I focused on my own career.

Nods went around the table. It seemed that "medical advancement" had some clout. The view of death depended on the goal.

I sacrificed many mice over several months and became more efficient with each experiment. I transformed from a squeamish, death-averse scientist to a dispassionate mouse killer. That transformation concerned me. I didn't like it. Retired after fifty years of science, I still think about these mice and believe strongly that one shouldn't be cruel to animals, even though that may make me inconsistent. I killed those mice. I no doubt would do the same today.

What I did find surprisingly consistent about my life, however, was how my character played out both in science and other activities, in particular, collecting.

The Collecting Bug

When I was about twelve years old, Grigory Gluckman, an artist and family friend, told my parents in my presence, "I see the Rothschild in Joram. He will be a collector. Just wait and see. I'm sure of it." Gluckman's instinct was right about my being a collector.

As a teenager, I unwittingly collected in my mind whatever I did. I considered my tropical fish (I wanted samples of the different types) and tennis victories (and sadly losses) as collections. Each science course I took in college was like another piece of my collected knowledge. As a scientist, I continued seeing my work as a collection. I filed chronologically my notes and slides I presented for the science lectures I gave, starting with my first at Caltech when I spoke to a junior high school class on sea urchin fertilization. I did the same for my journal club presentations in Leder's laboratory, and then for the presentations I gave in my own laboratory. I kept a series of notebooks of the science lectures I attended at conferences and elsewhere, and I've kept most of the books I've read on various topics, especially those related to science, with comments in the margins for future reference. I considered my 300 plus scientific articles, from the first on barnacles with Harold Barnes in Millport, when I was an under-graduate, to the most recent on perspectives of basic research, as if they were a collection. I believe seeing my work as a collection imposed a certain order on my research and contributed to my reluctance to undertake projects in which I didn't see a connection of some sort to a larger view of work.

Inheritance was a different matter. I inherited art– old master, impressionist and expressionist paintings, pottery, and other sculptural works – from my parents. Mama had inherited these precious items from her parents; Papa had bought the art himself. I loved my inherited art, both for its beauty as well as for its family connection. Pride in the art was pride in my family. But I didn't have a drive to enhance that art collection. Ironically, the inherited art interfered with collecting art myself. New additions would feel like poor cousins, and space was limiting. I felt as much a custodian of my inherited art as its owner. Also, I was as reluctant to sell any part of my inherited art, as I was to add to it. Selling would break the chain of a heritage I didn't build and couldn't replace. The loss of any piece would feel like losing a family member, not like a specific "hole" in the collection that needed replacement, or like having culled a piece to tighten the collection as a whole.

My inherited art reflected just a sliver of me; it glowed like a quarter-moon rather than its full body. It was like I had arrived at a destination before I left for the trip.

The collecting bug first bit me consciously when I was in my late forties. After spending the day skiing with Lona and my two sons in Vail, Colorado, I passed by a display of stone carvings in the window of the Alaskan Shop that attracted my attention. The Inuit pieces from central Arctic Canada seemed to be dancing in the display window and the movements caught my eye. I ambled into the store.

"Can I help you," asked the storeowner, Jim Robbins.

"I'm just browsing. Amazing things here."

Some of the carvings were green stone streaked with dark veins, and some black or dark grey stone; others were made from marine ivory or whalebone. The shop teemed with sculptures of Arctic life: caribou, polar bears, walrus and otters; family groups; wrestling figures; hunting and fishing scenes; women in childbirth; representations of Inuit myths – notably the Sedna, goddess of marine life – and shamanic transformations.

I'd never heard of the regions from which the different pieces originated in northern Canada, or the nearly unpronounceable names of the Inuit artists. I listened with one ear at best. It was as if a sexy lady had just appeared and a stranger started telling me where she was from, what her parents did for a living and what college she'd attended. Naturally my attention would be riveted on her – her smile, her curves, *her* charm – not her life history. And so it was with the sculptures. I gazed. I touched. They were inanimate objects, yet they were alive for me.

"This little Alaskan ivory bear is a beauty," I said, holding it in my hands. I liked its well-balanced feel and the fur represented by fine scratches on the surface. I replaced it on the shelf and left it waiting for another home. A few days later back in Bethesda, the image of that bear adhered like glue in my thoughts. If I'd seen it in a museum or in someone's home I probably would have forgotten it. But the notion of owning it – a tactile carving I'd handled carved by Dennis James-Gambell, who I'd never heard of – had nothing to do with intellect or investment. The yearning came from the gut, and it worried me. Was it irresponsible to squander money for what some might call an expensive trinket? What was driving me?

I bought the bear. Six months later I bought two other sculptures from the Alaskan Shop. A collecting seed was sprouting.

My son Anton gave me an Inuit sculpture of a kneeling caribou carved from lime-green serpentine for my fiftieth birthday. After that I bought an Inuit sculpture of a drum dancer (an activity often portrayed in Inuit carvings and prints), and then I bought many more sculptures, in galleries and in auctions. That snowball started an avalanche.

In contrast to inheriting art, purchasing Inuit art was my choice, my risk, and my opportunity to express myself through a novel art form. Collecting Inuit art gave me an identity in much the same way as doing research on the lens and crystallins. When I guided friends and guests through my art-filled home, the Inuit carvings glittered most brightly for me. The foreign names of the Inuit artists, the stories and myths that the sculptures expressed, where I'd bought the sculptures, how I imagined them interlocking artistically and culturally and, most importantly, with my interests and personality, all gushed from me like water from a broken dam. I became a leader rather than a follower within my heritage.

"Slow down, relax," my wife Lona often signaled me. I tried to comply, but seldom succeeded. I felt like a ventriloquist, projecting my voice as if it were part of the collection. The Inuit sculptures were not just carved stones from a foreign land; they were my adopted family, as I believe Papa felt about *Joli Garçon* – his adopted son, which even brought the artist, Soutine, into the fold.

To some extent, learning about esoteric Inuit art was driven by my character and interests, as when I took pride in learning the names of invertebrates in college that were foreign even to most scientists. Organizing names or objects of a specific kind into a coherent whole created a satisfying order, like classification in the animal kingdom. Establishing new and removing old boundaries was like whittling an essay into a coherent flow by organizing ideas. It had the quality of collecting.

Collecting, for me, wasn't limited to acquiring objects – it was a matter of character. Some people are collectors by nature, others aren't. Birders list the species they have observed in the wild; tourists aim to visit many countries; socialites brag about the number of celebrities they have met; lovers fill notebooks with the names of those they have seduced. These collections aren't objects.

My collecting Inuit art resembled my journey as a scientist. It was inherent in my character.

As my Inuit art collection grew, so did my appetite for enlarging it. Similarly, discoveries in research drove me back into the laboratory for more. I had no predetermined destination as I collected Inuit art or did research, no line to cross or amount that would satiate me. My Inuit art acquisitions were like my science publications: exhilarating moments that set the scene for more in the future.

Each piece of Inuit art told a story. The iconic migration carvings of the Inuit artist, Joe Talirunuili, depicted groups of starving Inuit packed in a sailboat searching for more productive hunting grounds. Each person in the boat represented a person in the artist's life. The subjects of Inuit sculptures were integral to their culture, such as family life, the importance of the group, the animals they hunted, the myths they believed, much as science fits into existing thought and knowledge at the time. The narratives of Inuit art blend with the aesthetics, each enhancing the other, shifting the collection as a whole with each new member. I viewed science the same way: each new finding shifted the narrative and pointed to new directions and possibilities.

Culling – deleting pieces – was a painful part of collecting, which took a bit of brutality. I confess culling made me feel sad or disloyal, and I did very little of it.

Collecting, like research, required the courage to risk mistakes. What collector wants to be branded with bad taste or low standards? What scientist wants to be known for oversights or being ignorant and careless? Selecting Inuit sculptures for my collection invoked risk, as did choosing a topic for research.

I recall an interview I had with a student writing a doctoral thesis on collecting. During our discussion, I compared collecting with research.

"Are you saying that collecting is the same as basic science research?" she asked, sounding skeptical.

"No, they're different, of course," I answered, feeling foolish for having stretched to tie the two activities together.

"Then why equate collecting and science?" She looked perplexed.

I had to dig deeply to explain. "Because I've been obsessed with both collecting and science," I answered. At that moment I realized that everything I'd said was personal, one point of view that would probably be refuted by another collector or research scientist.

"Obsessed?" she repeated.

"Yes. Collectors and researchers are both compulsive, obsessed," I said with more certainty than I felt.

"Is that what defines a collector? Obsession?"

I didn't know what to say.

"What influences what a collector collects?" she continued, ignoring that I had not answered her question about obsession.

"Well," I said, "I'm struck how often subject matter might reflect the collector's character and dreams."

"Character and dreams?" She perked up, seeming curious.

"Well, early on, the Rothschilds must have dreamed of making money and escaping the Jewish ghetto, which seems consistent with their initial collecting coins, and subsequently art. As for Papa, he devoted his life to music and concert halls, but he dreamed of going to the jungles that represented freedom; he bought tribal art from the jungles of Africa, and evocative paintings of Soutine and Cuevas, which went hand-in-hand with his personality, dreams and uncanny ability to see underlying truths."

"So, are you saying that it does matter what a collector collects?" my interviewer insisted.

I scratched my head. She was right. I was contradicting myself, but not completely. "Yes, what is collected does matter, but I don't believe that defines a collector any more than specific projects explains the passion of a researcher."

My interviewer looked at me quizzically, so I continued. "My friend Stanton, a forensic psychologist, loves schnauzers. He has one that he walks every morning, and he has amassed hundreds of objects connected with schnauzers: stuffed schnauzers, posters and pictures of schnauzers, written comments about schnauzers. My granddaughter Dalia, who was 9 at the time, thought Stanton belonged in the Guinness Book of World Records. What made him collect schnauzers? Was it love of the breed, his need to decorate his house with inanimate schnauzer-stuff, or just a diversion? Was it all three reasons, or none of them? I think Stanton's character was to collect, and it just happened to be schnauzers for him."

My answer was the best I could do at the moment.

"Well," she said, wrinkling her nose, "my goal today was to learn about collectors, not scientists or psychologists, so do you have any final words of wisdom about collectors before we conclude?"

"Do you mean that you still want some hints of why I collect Inuit art?"

"Yes," she said. "Why do you?"

I sighed. "Because I was ambushed by my character. Perhaps I'm just a collecting addict who needs my daily fix."

"An addict?"

"Who knows? Collecting may be encoded in my genes, or influenced by Papa's collecting what struck his fancy, or prompted by my Rothschild heritage of collecting. Maybe I collected Inuit art to leave a tangible trail, or maybe to realize a fantasy of living an alternate lifestyle in the far-off Arctic, like Papa dreamed of jungles, or maybe it was just interesting and artistically satisfying. Maybe it was all of those possibilities, or some of them, depending on the moment.

"But collecting would still be a part of my nature, not just a reflection of nurture. My sister was raised in the same environment as I and had the same heritage but didn't collect anything. I know only that collecting represents a personal expression, not someone else's, and that I derive daily pleasure from my sculptures, and still do. Each piece is a friend who speaks both to me and for me. Somehow, I need to collect."

I didn't say any more about science, but I was thinking I could have been describing my feelings and approach to research: I did it because it was interesting, I loved it, it was a personal expression and odyssey, and it identified me. It was in my character.

The interviewer prepared to leave.

"Thanks for taking the time to listen to me," I said, as I shook her hand.

Joram with Inuit sculpture collection, 2018.

I'm standing beside two Inuit sculptures by David Ruben concerning the
Sedna myth exhibited at the World Bank, 2018.

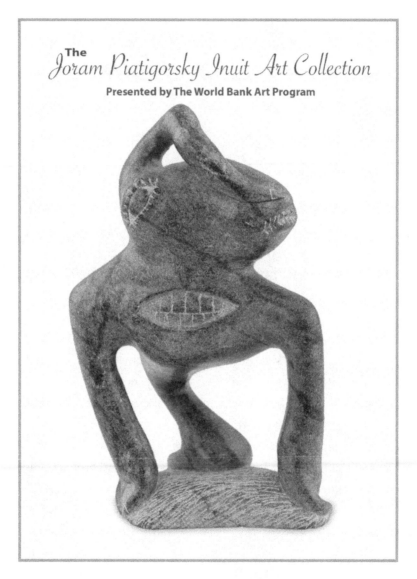

The
Joram Piatigorsky Inuit Art Collection

Presented by The World Bank Art Program

One of a series of cards made by Margaret Dimond for the Inuit Art
exhibition of my sculptures exhibited at the World Bank.
The fantasy sculpture (Spirit) is by Eli Sallualu, 2018.

Accordion of Time

The year I closed my NIH lab after fifty years of research, I traveled with Lona to the tiny hamlet of Lillooet, British Columbia, to visit my friend Van. I hadn't had any contact with him since high school. I sat in a comfortable armchair in my study in Bethesda the day after I returned to Bethesda and let my seventy-year-old mind become an accordion, contracting and stretching time from childhood to the present.

I imagined I was in my dress military uniform, a cadet of about 10 with the undistinguished rank of private at Black-Foxe Military Academy in Los Angeles. I was marching with boys from kindergarten to seniors on a rectangular grass field at one of the Friday afternoon parades. I never was the military type, but military schools had a good reputation after the war, and my parents approved of my going to school in a uniform wearing a tie, which was consistent with their formal European discipline. I stopped abruptly when the Lieutenant Colonel commanded, "BATTALION, HALT," and pivoted when he said, "LEFT FACE" – my heels joining the collective snapping sound.

I followed the others. If they turned left, I turned left. When I was a squad leader it was a different matter. If the leader said, "COLUMN RIGHT, OR COLUMN LEFT, MARCH," I had to turn in the correct direction, and the people in line behind me had to follow. I often got confused between right and left, because being left-handed, left was right for me, or something like that. Sometimes, then, I turned the wrong direction, creating confusion for the others. My remedy was to hold a small rock in my right hand, and keep in mind that the Rock was in the Right hand. It worked like a charm. It was a small issue in my life, but perhaps it foreshadowed my resistance to move with the herd.

Well, there I was at the Friday parade, standing motionless at attention, clutching an M1 rifle (without the firing pin) by my side, facing my parents on a bench across the field, when a small boy close to me fainted in the September heat. I wanted to help him, but I was not supposed to leave my place in ranks. I was a boy soldier. The sergeant, an upper classman, dragged the prone body off the field. I was scared of fainting myself.

"Wiggle your toes," I was told. "That will keep the blood circulating and prevent fainting."

I remembered wiggling my toes all day as well as during the parades to make sure I wouldn't faint. I never did.

The accordion of time stretches as I sit in my chair pondering my life. I'm a senior in high school and a major now, the executive officer on the staff of the battalion commander, the lieutenant colonel, the head honcho with six stripes on each arm. We both faced the battalion across the field, as he barked orders to the troops. I'm decoration, second in command, with five stripes on each arm. It was a perfect job for me then: a showcase with prestige, yet nothing to say or do except look pretty. I stood straight as a cornstalk thinking about my upcoming tennis match and worried that I messed up on the history exam that afternoon. I was preoccupied about getting into college.

My friend Van was a captain and stood at attention in front of Company B facing me.

I stretch the accordion to reach present time. Van appears as he was a few days ago with a gray beard and a ponytail, a man I never would have recognized if I didn't know he was my friend from way back then. He walked along the driveway to his home with his dog in beautiful Yalakom valley off the grid in British Columbia. I was in a rented car with Lona. I hadn't seen him in 52 years. Some say that's a long time. I don't know if I agree. I study evolution where serious intervals of time begin at hundreds of thousands, even millions of years. Van and I have lived entirely different lives, yet here we were together again, the gap between us temporarily closed.

"Joram," he said, "I can hardly believe you really came."

"Absolutely. It's great to see you again. Finally."

I didn't know what to expect from Van, gone hippie, with the courage and imagination to live an alternative lifestyle. I doubt that he knew what to expect from me either, a scientist from the U.S. government biomedical research laboratories in Bethesda. He lived by the rhythm of his whims; I punched a symbolic clock, at least until I closed my research lab last year and became an emeritus scientist. But now we were just two men in our seventies, both with beards, I rather bald, Van with a full head of hair. Lucky bastard!

Van showed us the vegetable garden and the storage place for winter food, and then the hot house where turkey chicks were maturing to become tasty meals. He stooped to care for the young ones, merging present love with future needs. He told me the only food he and his partner Eleanor bought was olive oil. Lona and I bought everything we ate. A cock strutted freely within the fenced yard. I think my fences have been self-induced by work and attitude. We reminisced about Black-Foxe, ate the homegrown vegetables, fresh eggs, turkey, Eleanor's jam, and goat cheese made by the neighbors, and then went for a short walk in the green paradise. I spotted an eagle high atop a tree – a mere white speck, free.

"Do you hear the crickets?" Lona asked.

I didn't. My hearing was fading. Age worried me. I had so much more to do.

Van's daughter, Robin, came by with her Cuban husband, Camilche, and their 6-month-old daughter, Osha, to spend the day with us. I thought of our two sons and their families living far from us, Auran in San Francisco and Anton in Toronto. A neighbor came by to do her laundry in Van's house.

"Hi," she said. "I won't be long." Van smiled at her.

Van lived modestly in a close-knit community. In Bethesda, a D.C. suburb, where we have lived for 35 years, we barely knew our neighbors.

Van's living room was lined with books on art, philosophy, travel, healing – you name it. There were more books in the adjacent study, where he produced his annual journal, *Lived Experience*, published locally. He had abundant time to read; I squeezed time to read for pleasure into a very busy schedule. I made a mental note to send him a copy of my book, *Gene Sharing and Evolution.*

Van showed me the deck with a mountain view where he was writing an autobiography. I imagine he had much to say, about leaving the United States where he grew up and going to British Columbia, living in a commune, owning several book stores in Vancouver, teaching literature at the University of British Columbia, raising his daughter Robin, becoming a grandfather, sustaining himself and Eleanor off the land in an interacting community, where water was as thick as blood.

I thought about my memoir in progress, still bits and pieces.

Van advised, "Keep writing about your life. Truth interests me more than fantasy."

I wondered what he imagined to be the difference between truth and fantasy, events, thoughts and dreams. For me, they blend and sustain each other.

Van remembered names and events from high school that I strained to recall. He mentioned his lawyer brother in Los Angeles, his college days at UCLA, his experiences in Cuba, travels in Europe, graduate school in Vancouver, his past life in the commune.

I sensed freedom with envy.

"It's a big industry, cutting down all those trees," he said out of nowhere.

"Around here?" Lona asked.

"Yes."

I heard a note of discouragement mixed with anger in Van's voice, all well controlled. He continued.

"I've spent so many hours fighting it. It's a relief to forget about problems and our community meetings for a couple of days."

I realized it's not the external environment that ultimately rules. Being at peace without problems was being dead. I was in no rush for that.

Eleanor offered hot tea.

I showed Van digital pictures on my laptop, hoping that my posh existence in suburbia wouldn't distance him from me, but it seemed not to. We were friends, after all; the rest was window dressing, like military rank at Black-Foxe.

As we talked I was struck by how we portrayed our lives as single stories, but there seems to be little truth in that. In fact, we had changed uniforms constantly, in our minds – sometimes from year to year, other times day to day. I thought of all the uniforms I'd worn: tennis player, student, research scientist, author, art collector, husband, father, grandfather and friend, trying to resolve all the layers of my life. Seeing Van again made clear that memories were more than footprints embedded in the past. Memories were more like movies with evolving plots than photographs; they were modified in different contexts and seen through different lenses under changing circumstances. Suddenly I realized that gene sharing – multiple uses for the same gene product – was no different from our lives of wearing many hats, depending on the time and circumstance. How beautifully the mosaic fit together!

I no longer saw Van as my high school friend in military school with greater military ambition. He was now a broader man in a softer cloth. I no longer saw my past confined to a scientist confronting nature's secrets, but as a period in my life that prepared me to cross borders and explore new pastures. And then the unexpected miracle: the memories transformed into the raw material for the narratives I was yet to write.

I was eager for the next phase of my life.

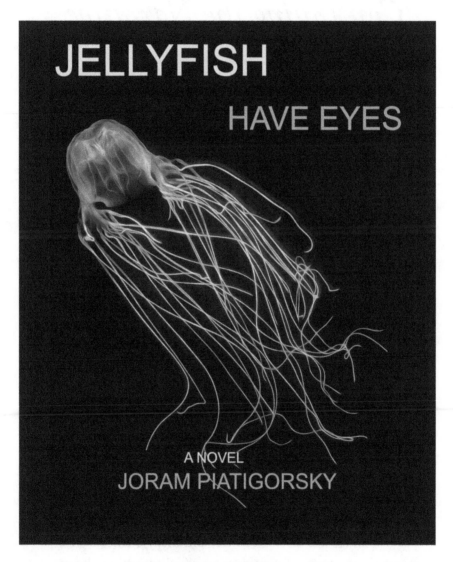

Jellyfish Have Eyes book cover.

Continuing the Narrative

I had never considered retiring. Science was my life and my identity for fifty years, and there was no age requirement for retirement at NIH. The administration could limit my laboratory space or budget for any number of reasons – declining research productivity, changes in the NEI mission, acquiring new technologies or hiring younger scientists to rejuvenate the Institute – but these weren't immediate threats to me. My laboratory was active, I was publishing articles in peer-reviewed journals, invited to give seminars, received applications for prospective postdoctoral fellows, and had an excellent review by the Board of Scientific Counselors, who had considerable influence on funding my lab.

Yet, I was 69 years old, frustrated with the consuming obligations that went with being a laboratory chief, and discouraged with the increasing emphasis on medically-oriented research rather than my brand of basic science. There were fewer and fewer seminars at NIH that interested me. Times were changing. Computer analysis, which was not my thing, was driving science, and many scientists were starting companies. The golden age of discovery was being replaced by a practical age of application and commerce, although, I admit, the remarkable advances in technology were exciting. However, when we identified a new DNA regulatory sequence controlling gene expression in the cornea, I felt more pressure to search for ways to implement its use medically rather than to trace its evolution or to delve into the complexity of how it regulated gene expression. In fairness, I never was asked to change my research direction, even when others in the NEI were urged to shift in one way or another. What had changed was the scientific climate.

Contemporary science had lost its luster and sense of adventure for me. Also, my bent to literature remained unsatisfied. I wanted to taste the freedom and challenge of writing on my own schedule and living the life of an artist, rather than continue as a government scientist managing a laboratory. I didn't feel pushed away from research; I felt pulled towards writing and more freedom. I hadn't diminished energy; I saw a different horizon.

But, conflict persisted. Closing my research laboratory felt like a defeat of sorts, like being a quitter. I believed that nothing could surpass or equal the beauty and imagination of nature, and being a scientist was a worthy intellectual challenge. I posed questions no one had before or knew the answers to, and I wanted to open doors no one knew existed. I should have been satisfied – proud, in fact. My research had shined a spotlight on the lens in the scientific community, as I had wanted it to do, and I believed gene sharing was an important conceptual factor of evolution, although I didn't think it had been fully appreciated yet by the science community, despite that it was represented in a number of textbooks and reviews. I had mentored my share of scientists who went on to successful careers in science. My laboratory established molecular biology as a critical part of the NEI and had garnered numerous recognitions. Most of my colleagues were surprised when I considered retiring from science.

When was enough, the same question I faced as a collector, haunted me, as always.

Conflicts wobble until a tipping point is reached. Then, sometimes, a single issue can resolve the matter. At the beginning of my career I decided to get a Ph.D. instead of a M.D. when I asked myself, "Would I prefer to study illness or health?" Without hesitation, health won the day for a Ph.D. Now I asked myself, "Would I prefer publishing more scientific articles or to stretch my imagination by writing novels, short stories and essays?" The latter made my adrenalin flow and challenged me in a new way. But could I succeed as a writer at my age, and would I accept being an amateur writer instead of a professional scientist? I could think of only one inconclusive answer, the same one I had when questioning whether I should become a scientist: don't judge the act before it's played.

I had no illusion that writing would be easy or even moderately successful for me. I knew writing was deceptively difficult and highly competitive, and any notion that a book would materialize – especially an interesting one – if I tapped out a story on my computer – was an absurd oversimplification that was expressed brilliantly in an anecdote I heard from my writing workshop instructor, Robert Bausch, a fine novelist.

"Bob, what did you do last summer?" asked a neurosurgeon.

"Oh, it was great. I finished a novel I'd been working on for a long time."

"Boy, you're lucky. I've always wanted to take a summer off and write a novel."

"That's some coincidence," said Bob. "I've always wanted to take a summer off to do some neurosurgery."

Really?

Writing was far more challenging than linking words together, however the consequences of a poorly received book were insignificant compared to a bungled surgery.

I decided to take a chance and closed my research laboratory in 2009, one month before my sixty-ninth birthday, and set forth into the world of writing, although my transition wasn't as abrupt as it sounds. Life seldom operates by crossing lines for the first time, and never by changing one's character or personality. My becoming a scientist was not a case of spontaneous generation; my career in science developed from seeds planted by my parents as much as by my inclinations. Papa influenced me by eradicating borders, which allowed me to be motivated by such unorthodox questions as, "What's the speed of dark?" Mama taught me that continual improvement – one step forward, then another, never ending – progresses to success, and her confidence in me boosted my confidence to become a scientist. But, these lessons applied as much to writing as to science. My transition from science to writing would change the landscape on my creative journey of exploration, but not my character or aspirations.

There was also another fact that I've failed to mention. I anticipated well before retirement from science that I might write later and figured that I should lay a writing foundation early on, since it would be far more difficult to start when I retired at an advanced age than to continue what I'd started earlier. Thus, I was 56 years old and in the midst of my scientific career when I first experimented with writing fiction. Lona and I were in Bar Harbor, Maine on summer vacation. We had hiked along a forested path and rested at a quiet spot with a scenic view overlooking a bay. Lona removed a pad of paper and pastel crayons from her backpack to sketch the scene. I leaned against a nearby tree hoping to open a new chapter in my life by writing a story or an essay. The problem was that I had no idea what to write about. My childhood? Science? Being on vacation?

"Just write! Anything!" I demanded, but no idea percolated. Opportunity swallowed my thoughts; the blank page threatened my imagination. Then I noticed that the thoughts jumping in and out of my mind didn't have equal weights. Some slid past as if escaping scrutiny, while others lingered, teasing me to explore their content. Each thought had a separate chemistry for me, as each window in a house exposed a different view, or as each scientific experiment raised a different question.

I recalled a similar difficulty in choosing a science project at the dawn of my graduate research at Caltech. No particular project stood out as compelling, nor would I have known how to go about doing the research if it had. I started learning techniques, step by step, thinking of various projects, until, with Tyler's help, I settled on studying protein synthesis in fertilized sea urchin eggs. Now, some 33 years later, what to write about seemed as challenging as choosing a research project.

As I pondered different possibilities for a short story, I thought of how being a scientist had unfolded in my life. My passion had developed gradually, from abstract faith to concrete reality. Perhaps writing required experimenting with words and ideas, as research depended on trial and error. Maybe the pen would move the story, not the other way around.

I started to write a story about an American teenage boy who went caribou hunting in the Arctic with an Inuit teenager – pure fiction stimulated by my interest in Inuit art. Each sentence prompted the next. The story progressed as if removing layers over covered treasure. Imaginary scenes of sunlit snow glittered in my mind. The plot didn't matter; there hardly was one. The teenagers sneaked out of my soul onto the page, ink flowed in their veins. How liberating to give birth to different characters hiding within me! I was doodling with words in order to create a paper world for me to inhabit, rather than mixing chemicals to describe the natural world.

After a couple of hours, the reddening sun perched on the horizon and I had written three pages. The boys, proud and ecstatic, had killed a caribou in the tundra. Elated, I wanted to write other stories, but I foresaw the common conundrum of not having enough time to write in my busy life of research. Science gobbled time without mercy. I decided to confine future writing to cracks of time, now and then, seizing whatever opportunities I could, but not overwhelm myself.

I became a short – very short – narrative specialist, limiting each story to what I could accomplish in a single sitting. My stories were neither polished nor publishable, but pages accumulated as I explored my thoughts and built a foundation for the future. I discovered that the frustration of stories that didn't work matched the frustration of experiments that failed, but neither prompted me to quit. Every sentence that successfully expressed my thoughts or feelings urged me on, as fresh data did in scientific research. Also, my stories, like research projects, concluded prematurely, or perhaps more correctly, never finished, since there were always more thoughts to develop, as there were more experiments to perform in research. I felt like a teenager again, but this time dreaming about writing rather than science.

I took evening workshops in fiction at The Writer's Center in Bethesda. As my writing skills developed, the differences between science and writing became more apparent. Right or wrong was meaningless in writing, while it was everything in science. Some critiques earmarked my favorite passages for deletion, while others preferred passages that I thought weak. Revision seemed always necessary, but there were no clear directions for revising a short story. Revisions in science targeted specific points requiring more information, usually another experiment. Writing abandoned me in the dark, groping for ideas to improve my stories.

The workshops I took became invaluable stepping stones into the community of writers. As a result of my taking a number of workshops, I was invited to join the board of directors at The Writer's Center. Although not wanting to become mired with administrative activities, being on the board gave me a writing home, which I clearly needed, and contributed to having a network of writers. The Writer's Center, being a nonprofit organization, existed from year to year by contributions, workshop fees and a few grants. It was a 'hand-to-mouth' organization. Thus, I started an endowment fund, which I hoped would enhance its independence and financial stability, like the Whitney Lecture endowment added to the stature of the Whitney Laboratory at the University of Florida.

My "borderless" views since childhood came into play. I was struck by how bare the cinder block walls were in The Writer's Center, and imagined that art would not only enhance the ambience, but also bring art into the world of writing, for writing is an art. Conversely, contributing artists might benefit by interacting with writers. I initiated art exhibits that rotated every three or four months at The Writer's Center. This promoted collaboration between artists and writers, and broadened the scope of the writers, and hopefully, of the artists. Art again. This time it was for writing instead of science or collecting.

As my writing progressed, similarities with a life in science crept in. Writing may be a solitary activity, but it thrives on the exchange of ideas and constructive critiques, as does science. My challenge in writing was to navigate through the morass of differing opinions and to become a messenger from the heart, where omission was as important as inclusion, and implication as vivid as explanation. This contrasted with criticism in science, which was more to point out what was in error or needed further experiments. As a writer, I strived to open space for the reader to enter the story, while as a scientist, I aimed for clarity to fill space, leaving the reader outside of the subject.

I generally began a story with a blurred idea. Once, I started a story about a character whose favorite activity was standing in line, and I had no clue how it would play out. This was not unlike when I started a science project. I may have had expectations for experimental results, but I was often fooled. I didn't know where my experiments would take me. Each science project invariably fractionated into multiple projects with increasing data, as each story required continual decisions to move one way or another. Science didn't compromise, and neither did the fictional characters in my stories. In contrast to science, however, I didn't need to qualify every speculation with caveats. I had to pay more attention to consistency and have the characters earn their traits. Initially, writing acted as a foil to science that gave me an opportunity to express internal, personal truths rather than seek dispassionate, external facts.

As time progressed, I started writing longer stories, many of which wandered beyond my experiences. One story was about a man who didn't realize he was dead, and a sequel was about a man who thought he was dead but was delighted to learn that he was still alive. In a science-fiction story, I traveled to a distant planet populated by clouds with human qualities that communicated with invented words. In still a different tale, I questioned whether an ugly person could be elected president. I thought that could never happen in our democracy, until my protagonist – a repulsive, very smart woman lawyer – campaigned on the platform of banning mirrors. People had to look at each other rather than at themselves, an idea that evolved as I was writing the story, and she was elected.

The more I wrote, the more I saw fiction relying on fact, but I also became aware of how much science relied on narrative and speculation. Neither science nor writing were all fact or all fiction.

"How can that be?" asked a friend. "Science is factual, not a story, and your stories certainly aren't fact or reality."

"Really?" I muttered, thinking of how I could respond.

"Absolutely," she continued. "DNA is a double helix. How's that fiction or a narrative?"

She had a valid point, so I considered how to defend my position. "Science strives for a temporary truth within a narrative medium," I said, on a quest for what I meant.

I sensed that she wasn't going to agree with any argument I made, so I tried to convince myself rather than her. I argued that science is part truth, part narration – a merger of two worlds – like good literature.

"Why," I asked her, "would a scientific theory often need to be modified when new data became available to produce a consistent narrative, if the current view of nature wasn't partially speculative?"

This was consistent with my belief that research interpretations were fragile and tentatively woven together as the story progressed. Some characters (proteins or other biochemicals) might have been missing, while others may have been included that might not belong. The narrative constantly evolved with new observations and experimentation.

Consider DNA genes – the templates for embryonic development and at the heart of evolution – that my skeptical friend brought up. I wrote a 27-page chapter ("The

Elusive Concept of a Gene") in *Gene Sharing and Evolution* to touch upon the changing views of a gene throughout history. These holy grails of biology went from being minuscule humans (a homunculus) within spermatozoa in the seventeenth century, to being an undefined state or condition that specifies particular cellular properties, to being imaginary cellular particles that are partitioned during embryonic development. Later, with more data available, a gene was defined as a continuous stretch of DNA nucleotides that encodes a particular protein, until it was shown that most genes were more complex, with its DNA sequence interrupted numerous times with stretches of nucleotides – introns – that didn't have any information specifying the protein the gene encoded. In short, genes were both continuous and stitched together and had more information content than understood. Genes in pieces! What next?

Thanks to the presence of introns, the early dogma that one gene encoded a single protein was superseded by the discovery that a single gene could produce a group of related proteins, by including or excluding certain pieces of the protein encoded in the DNA template, a process that stems from alternative RNA splicing. Antibody genes even restructure themselves in response to protect efficiently against diverse infections, from a cold to pneumonia. And then there was gene sharing: genes made proteins with multiple functions. The story continued:

Genes were considered chemically invariant, but soon thereafter it was shown that the DNA could be chemically modified with functional consequences (starting the field of epigenetics). Moreover, many genes didn't code for proteins at all, but had regulatory functions that were still being explored. Even lumping together all the genes we know accounted for much less than half of the bulk of our DNA genes, and that's giving an overly generous portion to known activity. In other words, we're still speculating on the functions of most of our genetic material and continuing to write the gene story.

Few scientists today would agree with a single definition for a gene. I would not. How will a gene be defined in the future? How will the gene narrative change? For the story to conclude, it would require that we know everything about our DNA and genes so that no more speculation would be necessary. But, of course, we never know what we don't know, so the story can never be considered complete.

"Okay, science is an evolving truth," my friend conceded. "But I still have trouble relating science to narrative."

Instead of trying to define science as narrative rather than fact, I changed tactics and asked her to venture on an imaginary trip to Egypt where she would take photographs – collect data like a scientist – in order to give a travelogue to her friends. But, how would she choose what to photograph, or how would she interpret the photographs conceptually? Did she have a story in mind that she illustrated with photos? How would she modify that story as different images accumulated? Did she know what occupied the minds of the people she photographed, what personal problems they had, who they represented within the society, or whether they considered themselves privileged or underdogs? When she photographed the pyramids, what did she know about the lives of the slaves who built them? She could make educated guesses that made sense with what she saw and the fragments of information she had, but she would be speculating on incomplete information. Her evolving story would be limited to her observations and truth about Egypt gleaned from her photographic data coupled with other bits of information at her disposal. Her story would not be identical to someone else's who took different photographs or interpreted them on the basis of having had different experiences or from a different perspective. Writers – alias tourists – and scientists both draw incomplete conclusions from incomplete and different sets of data, filling in along the way, combining facts with speculation and/or fiction, creating a consistent narrative.

"So," I told my friend, "neither science nor stories of any genre – biographies, historical novels and, of course, fiction – escape our imagination. Data, referenced documents and memories – the facts of science and literature – are sprinkled with speculation to create believable narratives."

That research observations differing from expectation are viewed skeptically is consistent with the conservative nature of science. However, I was surprised when similar skepticism of my short stories drew such critiques as, "That couldn't have happened," or "That's not believable," or "That's too coincidental," even if the story had borrowed largely from events that had happened! I asked Robert Bausch why true happenings in life might not be accepted as plausible in fiction.

"Because," he said, "a writer must account completely for the causes of events in a story. There must be consistency to be believable."

"Just like a scientist must find believable causes for phenomena?" I added.

"Correct. All events in real life have causes, whether or not we know them. In fiction, there's nothing else but the story. The author is responsible for everything. Fiction can't conjure inconsistent happenings – create events solely for the convenience of the writer to solve problems."

I understood. A writer couldn't invent an inconsistent event to solve a dilemma in fiction, as a scientist couldn't fabricate data to satisfy a theory. Fiction and science require some connection with previous experience in order to succeed.

After retiring from science, I focused on expanding my novel, *Jellyfish Have Eyes*, which had languished in my computer for ten years. I went to the Helen R. Whiteley Center – a place for scholars of different persuasions to do creative work of their choice – at the University of Washington campus in Friday Harbor on Puget Sound to work on my novel. Friday Harbor was familiar territory since I'd spent a summer there during my graduate school days doing research on sea urchin fertilization with Arthur Whiteley as my mentor. He had established the Whiteley Center in honor of his deceased wife, a scientist with broad interests. Science and writing spoke to each other for me there, and it was a perfect place to delve into writing my novel. Arthur Whiteley, 94 years old, was still there keeping up with science and able to share ideas with me. I was joining two strands of my life, eliminating borders.

Jellyfish Have Eyes, set fifty years in the future, merged science with fiction.*(47)* The protagonist, Ricardo Sztein, speculated that jellyfish interacted with one another, had a brain of sorts, and visualized evolution – my imagination veering towards science fiction. The novel forewarned of the danger to creativity if funding for medical research swamped out that for basic research, precisely what I had worried about as a scientist. Now I wrote about it as a novelist. The science and writing paths crossed. I was gratified when the science writer, Joel Shurkin, reviewed the novel in the Proceedings of the National Academy of Sciences and agreed with my use of fiction to make the case for basic research.*(48)*

Nothing was left behind as my life moved along, I didn't shed my skin; I built upon my life, which was driven by background and character. Growth related more to recognizing and accepting myself than to imagining that I had become someone else.

It took a while for me to recognize that my choice to collect Inuit art was in the same mold as my choices in research. My preference for Inuit carvings of shaman transforming into various species was linked with my interest in evolution. Carvings of shamanic transformations mixed diverse animal bodies (caribou, bears, muskox, birds) with faces or limbs or feet of humans, or alternatively, mixed animal ears or wings or hoofs or claws or antlers with human bodies. Sculptures of bears or muskox or caribou with human postures represented more subtle transformations. What biologist would not treasure such imaginative creatures? I saw transformations between species in Inuit carvings as artistic representations of evolutionary continuity among animals, humbling the idea of human superiority, and reflecting a deep and unwavering equality and respect for all species. I have connected these thoughts with my science by adding a photograph of an Inuit sculpture of a shaman as the frontispiece of *Gene Sharing and Evolution*. My Inuit art collection is an outgrowth and expression of my love of science.

I recently recognized another link between my research and collecting Inuit art: obscurity, escaping the crowds, living Frost's famous poem, *The Road Not Taken*. I sought the road "less traveled by" and, yes, "that has made all the difference."

Inuit art is almost unknown among artists, collectors, galleries and auction houses. The names of the Inuit artists are foreign and difficult, almost impossible, for us to pronounce. Who has heard of Judas Ullulaq (Ooloolah) or Barnabas Arnasungaaq? Who can locate Igloolik or Baker Lake on the map? Except for a very small group of Inuit collectors, no one. Inuit artists are virtually unknown to art critics and scholars. All art lovers recognize a Renoir painting or Giacometti sculpture and know well that Paris and Rome were major historical art centers. I equate these famous artists, and the hot new artists in the art market, to the so-called "bandwagon" in science, the populated fields watched and appreciated by everyone. Don't misunderstand me. Bandwagon fields are popular for good reason: they're filled with wonderful artists and key scientists from whom we benefit. They impact our views. But I found it satisfying - even creative - in learning to link the obscure names of Inuit artists with their little-known work in the distant and frigidArctic, as I was drawn to shadows hidden from popular glare by studying the eye lens of invertebrates, including jellyfish.

As an Inuit art collector, I was a scientist. As a scientist, I was a collector. My penchant for crossing borders, blending identities, was instilled in me by my family when I was a boy, making science and writing and collecting art all fit under the same umbrella.

The scientist in me argues that a collection requires some unifying rationale to meld the collection together, much as an evolutionary tree joins disparate species, or linked essays relate a common theme. Disconnected objects do not comprise a collection in the same sense in my opinion. Even displaying the pieces in a coherent context makes a significant difference. When my home was renovated, and the sculptures were stored as in a warehouse, stuffed here and there wherever they fit safely, my Inuit collection lost its appeal. Disorganization can harm a collection as much as organization and display can enhance it. Collecting requires order, as does science, as does literature.

Whether researching, writing or collecting, I have tried to navigate the turbulent seas of creativity and have struggled with the impossibility of touching bottom or reaching shore. I had no destination to reach, no rules that had to be followed or boundaries that I couldn't cross, which made my life infinitely challenging and never complete.

I still hear the accordion of time merging my past with the present, playing tunes as the Pied Piper, tempting me to follow into the future. There's more to do, but it's late and I'm sleepy. I'll close my eyes and rest awhile and continue my journey tomorrow along the circle of my life.

Papa

Lung cancer from a lifetime of smoking cigarettes poisoned my last memories of Papa. After being diagnosed, he pretended to stop smoking, but in fact he continued in private from time to time.

"Look," he said, "I've smoked my whole life. Stopping now would be a shock to my lungs and more dangerous than continuing."

He didn't have a death wish. That was just the way his mind worked. "There's nothing better than life," he had said repeatedly, and he fought to stay alive. He refused to accept he had cancer, yet at the same time, I believe he knew exactly that he did.

"I'm a survivor," he claimed, trying to convince himself that his cancer was an invisible combatant that he could defeat, as he survived pogroms in Russia and escaped Hitler in Europe.

But denial or false hope would not work, and the lung surgery he had didn't cure him. The cancer had metastasized. Yet, he continued to ask, "But what's wrong with me?" when his physician and friend, Dr. Lailee Bakhtiar, told him directly how advanced his cancer was.

It would have been exasperating, if it weren't so sad.

Antonio Stradivari   page 135

"The Batta" (1714)

The most magnificent Violoncello in existence — a unique masterwork, which should be preserved for all time for art & loving humanity. After I am gone it still be intrusted in to the hands of my beloved son Joram, who I know will cherish this great instrument as much as I did. "The Batta" was bought for Joram (& be signed by me) and as the owner, he is now to will it known as "The Piatigorsky — ex Batta Stradivari.

Gregor Piatigorsky
Los Angeles, Aug. first 1961.

my advise to Joram is, should he desire to sale this Stradivari he must be assured that the new owner will be capable of taking care this priceless instrument likewise. Unfortunately only a few great Violoncellists can be trusted in keeping fine instruments in meticulous order. Father.

Papa's willing his Stradivarius cello to me

292

Papa continued performing and teaching until the end. I was with him in Philadelphia when he played the Brahms double concerto with Isaac Stern. He was too weak to get out of the bathtub by himself before the concert, yet he appeared on stage in the Robin Hood Dell Music Center in Philadelphia, an outdoor amphitheater, with his cello held high – his trademark – as he walked across the stage to applause. He held his own until the last note, forcing an extra surge of energy to overcome the noise of airplane engines passing above.

Instead of the usual reception or gathering of admirers and music lovers after a concert, Papa went directly back to his hotel in a taxi. Although drained of energy, he felt proud to have made the effort. He may not have defeated cancer, but he proved to himself that he was indeed a courageous survivor. My memory of Papa at that moment is fixed in my mind, and I can only hope that when my time comes, I can emulate his strength.

Despite his seriously weakened state, he went to teach a summer master class at Montreux, Switzerland. We made it into a family affair. I wonder what Papa thought of the invasion, including Mama and the families of Jephta and me. We even brought Nancy along, our neighbor babysitter, for help with Auran and Anton, both under five years old. There were about twenty-five suitcases involved!

Papa pushed himself each day without complaining. When his course ended, he was too depleted to travel from Montreux back to his home in Los Angeles, so he stopped halfway at my home in Bethesda to rest. We had just bought a new house, making Mama and him our first guests. He stayed two days until he gained enough strength to finish the journey to Los Angeles.

Shortly after he had returned home, and the end was imminent, I went to Los Angeles to see him one last time. Although bedridden, he was still advising students, who came to see their maestro.

He made the effort to walk with me in the yard among the fruit trees he always loved – his orchard, as he called it. As we ambled along, he mentioned that his address book was filled with corpses. He never said that he was about to join them, but the message was clear. He did not speak about his professional or personal life – his satisfactions or disappointments or regrets – and I didn't quiz him. I too found it difficult to speak intimately about myself. I listened. I especially regret that I didn't say that I loved him. Papa's imminent death propelled neither of us into a different reality than the one that existed throughout my life as a child or an adult. Our most intimate feelings, deep as they were, remained somewhere in the gap between us.

What I remember best of our talk was his statement, "You will need to prepare yourself to lead the family in the years ahead."

"What do you mean?" I asked. Did he mean my immediate family, since there was nothing new in that, or my extended family, who didn't need me?

"You'll see," he said. "You must be strong, and I know you will be."

Perhaps my paraphrasing what Papa said forty-two years ago is not exactly verbatim, but it's what I remember.

Papa died a couple of days after I had returned to Bethesda, and so, once again, I flew to Los Angeles, this time with Lona, the day he died. Jephta and Dan were already there. As soon as I entered the house, Mama took me upstairs to see Papa's dead body before the morticians arrived to take it to the morgue. His eyes were closed as a drawn curtain: no humanity could penetrate or reach out. He wasn't Papa anymore.

I recoiled internally a bit when I first saw his dead body. Mama, who stood next to me and noticed everything, took my hand and placed it on his. What I felt was more leather than skin. She said that she wanted me to feel the distance, to understand that he was gone, to accept his death. Mama didn't deal with euphemisms.

Papa had a memorial service at the Bovard Auditorium at the University of Southern California, where he and Jascha Heifetz held master classes. The service was more a tribute to him as the world-renowned cellist than a personal expression of his life or feelings of those who loved him. Since Papa wasn't religious and didn't belong to a synagogue, we arranged for Rabbi Magnum, a well- known rabbi in Los Angeles, a stranger to us, to lead the service. Itzhak Perlman played his golden violin, accompanied by Doris Stevenson, Papa's assistant in his master class and loyal friend of many years. There were no personal eulogies that touched me. I didn't speak at the service, nor did Mama or Jephta or any other family member. The memorial was a ceremony for his public, not his family. From my viewpoint, it fluttered in the gap between us.

It was thirty-six years later when I attended Mama's memorial service and funeral that I fully realized the absence of intimacy of Papa's memorial. We all gave eulogies at Mama's service, including her five grandsons and a few close friends and associates. Her many accomplishments were noted; however, it was her human qualities and many acts of kindness and generosity that were stressed. I remember Auran and Anton, and then Jephta and Dan's children, my nephews Jonathan, Evan (who honored her with his cello) and Eric, each speaking about their grandmother with touching maturity, modesty and intelligence, turning my sadness to pride in my family.

I recognize that celebrities of great accomplishment like Papa are viewed as special and float on a higher plane than ordinary folks, which is reflected in public occasions, including their own memorial service. Regardless of his fame or accomplishments, however, Papa was very much a human being with shortcomings and endearing foibles, like the rest of us, like me. I recall this human side of Papa – the private person and father – in my mind now, many years after his death.

Driving was one of Papa's shortcomings. He never drove until relatively late in life; he was chauffeured everywhere by Mama, by his students, by his fans, by anyone willing with a car. At about fifty, however, he decided it was time to become independent and took driving lessons, obtained a driver's license and bought a car. I commend him for the courage to learn to drive so late, but oh my god! First, he never made a left turn to not risk being hit by a car going through the intersection. The one time he did turn left, an oncoming car broadsided him. Fortunately, he escaped with only a bruised leg. As might be expected, refusing to turn left took him astray. I remember when he was on one of his car excursions, he called to say he was hopelessly lost and would be late coming home. Big surprise! Eventually he reappeared after a series of strategically executed right turns. I doubt that he could have retraced the path he took.

Then there was the time he flooded the street by colliding into a fire hydrant. He quickly drove home, only a block away, before anyone noticed the disaster, and walked back to the scene of the crime to find out what had happened. This was hardly the famous cellist bowing to applause.

Luckily, Papa never had a serious accident, despite that he often drove too fast and tended to confuse the accelerator for the brake. Once he rammed through the back wall of the garage, resulting in the front of the car projecting towards the front lawn. Lona and I remained on high alert when Papa was on the loose in his car, worried about Auran or Anton playing in the driveway when they were very young.

Another time, attempting to parallel-park, he couldn't understand why the rear of the car in front of him was rising as he continued to accelerate when his bumper was beneath it. To make matters more interesting, a woman in the rising car got out, no doubt furious, and recognized Papa.

"Mr. Piatigorsky. What an honor to meet you! No bother. It's an old car. No harm done. Really. I'm such a big admirer of yours."

He probably gave her an autograph.

When Papa returned from concert tours, tired, he engaged little in daily life. Home was his refuge to recharge for his next concert tour, which was always around the corner. He neither puttered around the house nor shared family chores, such as grocery shopping or putting Jephta and me to bed when we were little or helping us with our homework. Maybe that was for the best. As for math, never having attended elementary school in Russia, he multiplied by adding a column of the same number repeated as often as necessary. That would not have helped us get good grades!

I was told he started a small fire (quickly extinguished) when he tried to fix an electrical plug on a lamp in Elizabethtown.

Papa did have good intentions, however. There was the time Mama was bedridden with the flu and she asked him to boil an egg for her.

"Sure," he said.

After the water was heating on the stove a while, he rushed from the kitchen to the bedroom to ask her what to do when the water spat bubbles in the air. Neither kitchens nor boiling water were his things.

Never mind. Papa was a formidable and charismatic personality with a strong presence for me, whether home or away.

I have been asked repeatedly if I played the cello or any musical instrument, as if it would be strange if I didn't. The answer was more complex than the question. I had a few piano lessons when I was very young and attempted the clarinet as a teenager, while Jephta made steady progress on the flute. Apart from listening, music did not come naturally to me in any form. I never could bring myself to sing or carry a tune publicly or even privately for my ears only when I was in the shower! I faked chanting with the congregation in synagogue at the High Holy Days, which I attended occasionally after I got married.

Once, when Papa returned from a concert tour, I proudly played with Jephta a short duet for him, she on the flute and I on my B-flat clarinet. I didn't hear the need to transpose. In any case, playing exactly in tune was overrated as far as I was concerned. It didn't help that my mother had her own conflicts with music, never having succeeded to her satisfaction when learning piano growing up. She insisted that perfect pitch was essential to play music.

"I don't have the 'perfect pitch' gene," she said about herself.

I didn't either. She never considered that pitch could be trained to some extent, certainly enough to be an amateur musician for pleasure. Why was "perfect" always necessary? I don't remember what Papa said about our duet that day, except that it was not more than a few words, if even that. What I do recall is that I didn't play the clarinet again. Jephta did continue with the flute and played chamber music with friends for many years. The irony was that her husband Dan, a neurologist, was a fine clarinetist.

Despite it all, I still wanted to play a musical instrument. One day I approached Papa with my latest brainstorm.

"What about the oboe?" I asked.

I have no notion why I considered playing that instrument. The idea came out of nowhere. I didn't know anyone who played the oboe and I never listened to recordings of the oboe. At least Lona knew why she had chosen to play the French horn when she was in high school: it was the only instrument that was missing from the school band, so she could fill an empty niche.

"Ridiculous!" Papa said. He didn't ask why I suddenly came up with the idea to play the oboe.

"A double reed instrument is impossibly difficult and not for you."

"Learn the recorder," he suggested. "Music is music, whatever instrument is played. The recorder is more realistic for you and less time consuming. You could have a lot of fun playing with other amateur recorder players."

He made sense, yet I procrastinated for several years. When I was a postdoctoral fellow at the National Institutes of Health and had some time to explore new interests, I signed up with a recorder instructor at a local music school attended mostly by school kids. I don't know whether to laugh or cry, or both, when I recall those lessons. There was a bench in the entrance of the school for students waiting for their turn. Imagine the feeling of being in my mid-twenties, the son of one of the most famous cellists in the world, clutching my wooden alto recorder, barely able to read music, squeezed between pre-high school children holding their violins, clarinets, trumpets, whatever instruments they had chosen, yes, even oboes, preparing to join the school orchestra or band. Swallowing my pride, I persisted and learned enough to play chamber music for recorders with friends for several years, which I enjoyed a great deal. Not a glorious triumph, but not a failure either.

Papa wasn't always tactful, but he was often right.

I imagine that music for me was analogous to science for Papa. Papa was drawn to nature, which he equated to science, in the same way that I listened to music: for the beauty and inspiration. Science became my world with boundaries that set me apart from him, like music was his universe that set him apart from me. Neither of us successfully crossed those barriers between us. Surprisingly, music was not discussed at home. All I knew about music beyond its beauty was tidbits floating in the breeze, which wasn't much, despite that I was raised in the midst of the finest musicians of the times.

I asked Papa once if he didn't get bored playing the same compositions repeatedly as he concertized.

"It's a re-creative art," he said. "Every time it's a little different, and each phrase requires interpretation. When the composer specifies allegro or andante, or variations of tempo, I have to decide how fast or how slow, and so on."

I thought of my research, and how I worked on the same problem for years and gave similar lectures using the same illustrations repeatedly. Each time, like Papa, I made small additions or deletions or modifications. The lectures were never precisely the same, at least for me. Scientists or artists rarely have truly new ideas; they massage what they have and make modest alterations. These changes, however, are not insignificant. A small bend can make a large difference in direction and destination. Perhaps Papa the cellist and I the scientist had more in common than we recognized, but we didn't talk about that. The gap between us, or at least the gap that I felt, prevented us from taking full advantage of each other.

I wish I had another chance.

I was in awe of his musical ability. I remember a social evening of chamber music with the pianist Leonard Pennario among friends of my parents. When we drove home, Papa commented that he had never heard one of the compositions they had played.

"It's a fantastic piece," he said.

"How's it possible you've never seen or heard it?" I asked, finding it hard to believe it was his first contact with the composition. "You had your eyes closed when you were playing it."

"Yes, I know. I looked ahead a bit as the piece progressed."

Sight-reading without looking!

And then there was the time when he was scheduled to play the Schumann cello concerto in an upcoming concert. He told me that he hadn't played that piece for fourteen years.

"But I haven't heard you practice," I said.

"Well, I practiced the fingering in my mind when lying in bed."

Was that analogous to my visualizing my slides in the order I was going to present them before an upcoming science lecture I was going to deliver? Is my remembering published data from articles I read some time ago similar to remembering the notes of a concerto? Does it make any sense to compare different disciplines or fathers and sons?

Thoughts of science or writing, or whatever preoccupies me at the moment, often creep into my mind when I'm at a concert. I value the opportunity to sit and think without being disturbed for a few hours, sometimes more than the music itself. More often, the music synergizes with my thoughts and makes them sharper, as if stimulating one part of the brain activates other parts.

I have a special weakness for opera, especially the lyrical 19th century Italian operas by Bellini, Donizetti, Verdi, Puccini and Rossini. I'm amazed how a singer can hit the right note with only an ear for guidance, a sense of what's correct, without the crutch of a fingerboard for string instruments or keys for woodwinds. Also, voice in opera is direct and personal, like a story told in the first person without the messenger of an instrument. Opera transcends plot, with music providing the impact, as prose does for a novel.

The first opera I attended was *La Bohème* with Jephta when we were teenagers in Los Angeles. After Mimi concluded her dying aria, tears rolled down our cheeks. Words failed to convey the emotional impact I felt. Jephta and I sent the tenor Jan Pierce (sometimes spelled Peerce), whom Papa knew, a telegram saying how moved we were by his performance. Music had a personal connection for me due to Papa, even if I didn't know the musicians and couldn't play an instrument. He brought a sphere of influence in the world of music to our family that I felt included me, as much as I felt at other times excluded.

I don't remember Papa ever going to an opera, saying that he disliked music being diluted with acting. He was a musical purist. Background music especially was distasteful to him. He equated music crammed into his ears when he entered a restaurant to having food stuffed into his mouth without permission by a waiter.

While Papa's sense of humor was legendary, his music was deadly serious and intensely personal. He believed that every time he played for others was a performance and that every public exposure was like a professional event, even if the public comprised only friends in social occasions. In his opinion, everyone judged, everyone counted; no audience was impartial, ever, even if there was no immediate consequence of note. His personal standards were paramount, a lesson I found applicable to every phase of my life. Compromises were not acceptable, and standards needed to be maintained.

Already as a boy in Russia practicing in private on his cello he soaked his hands in ice water, training himself to overcome unexpected difficulties – physical obstacles – that might occur during a performance. He went to rehearsals in a coat and tie, regardless of the heat or humidity or informality of the occasion, to mimic the concert attire to prepare for constraints that might occur during the performance.

"You don't play concerts in shirtsleeves," he said.

Papa was a harsh critic, especially for himself, and surprisingly sensitive to criticism for a man of his professional stature. He took personally even a single disparaging phrase by a music critic in an otherwise favorable review. I have seen him buy a stack of newspapers to prevent others from access to a review he disliked. Futile? Naturally, but it was an expression of pain, not logic or conceit or arrogance.

"It's like a cat scratching my eyes out," he'd say despondently. How he suffered!

Critics could also enrage him. Ignorance judging knowledge! Amateurs teaching professionals! Outrageous! He told me of a critic who wrote a review without attending the concert, and of another who had been recently promoted from sports to music. (Not everyone would consider that a promotion.) I can still hear my father's ire some forty years after his death: "How dare they tell me how to interpret the score!"

"Why do you take them so seriously?" I asked. "A review is just one person's opinion, and not even all the critics agree. Opinions vary."

"Because critics determine public opinion," he'd rationalize. "It's their voice that establishes success or failure in our profession. No colleague ever comes to the rescue of a musician stung by a critic's pen. It's too dangerous for their future. The critics wield a great deal of power over us artists."

"Hold on," I said. "No critic can eliminate the standing ovation, the applause, the appreciation and recognition from that very same public that may (or may not) read the reviews."

Papa understood this, and he knew his strengths. He knew that his sensitivity to critics was personal and that critics need not be musicians to comment on a performance, that objectivity of distance often clears the fog of subjectivity, that critics evaluate the performance, not the person, and that they often have a worthwhile point of view. He too had interesting opinions and views of subjects in which he had less than professional knowledge. But as great a musician as he was, he had his insecurities, like the rest of us.

What insecure creatures most of us are, being so sensitive to criticism and allowing critics to set the standards.

We flock to movies that are celebrated by four stars and skip those marred by less than two. We read books reviewed favorably and that win awards and let the others collect dust. We reluctantly praise that which critics pan. Rather, we strain to agree, which is safe – if you can't beat them, join them – except for those few individuals who may attempt to hide their insecurity by contradicting critics. I knew a scientist who prefaced every comment with a caveat of caution, and a philosopher who predictably responded with, "I don't agree."

But the issue here is not critics per se: it's the effect of critics on the performer. Artists live in a circular world with a porous perimeter. Imagine standing in the middle of that private space where we experience dreams and struggle with our doubts when an imposter trespasses through the pores to expose us. I understood Papa's personal reactions, for I too can no more ignore or forget criticism or be insensitive to its nasty residue than I can cling to the comfort of praise.

Despite the gap in intimacy, Papa was special, an original; no other father would have been comparable. I treasure Papa's inscription on the picture of us on a boat on a fishing trip in San Diego, grinning broadly at each other. I'm holding a strange-looking creature. The inscription reads, "To my only son and the best pal with tender love from his best friend and only Father." It's dated February 4, 1955, my fifteenth birthday.

And then there is *The Adventures of Huckleberry Finn* that Papa gave me when I was seven. On the inside cover

Papa wrote: "To Joram Piatigorsky with tender love from his father. Elizabethtown, 1947." Papa also gave me *Of Whales and Men* by R. B. Robertson, a book related to the sea that I realize only now I've never read. It's eerie how he saw me linked with marine biology already when I was fourteen. The inscription inside the book reads, "To the finest boy in the world my son Joram from his loving Father. 1954."

My heart breaks when I reread these loving inscriptions. I sense a self-consciousness that was no less in him than in me. He referred to himself as "his father" and even used my last name in his inscription when I was seven years old.

Papa often called me "Sonshine." I called him Papa when I was a very small boy. As I grew older, I referred to him as Father, not Papa, when I spoke to Jephta or Mama about him. "Dad" just wasn't in our European vocabulary. When I spoke to him as an adult, I didn't call him anything – neither Papa nor Father. When I wrote, I called him Father, as stiff as that felt.

It's that gap again, the space created by the numerous absences of his concertizing, the music I never played, the science he never understood, the Russian I didn't know, the childhood in peaceful America he never had, the pogroms I never endured or the war I never escaped, the secure future I was given but that he had to earn by his wits, talent and courage.

Yet, Papa was my "only Father," and I his "only son," as he wrote on the photo. We each occupied a unique and indispensable part of each other. There may be more conventional fathers, but I can't imagine one that could give me more than he did in his own fashion. Papa continues to inhabit my mind as a part of me that makes me who I am, no less than my heart or brain or soul.

I don't regret that I wasn't musical, but rather the difficulty I had in expressing my feelings for Papa. I regret how little I've done for him or how little credit I ever gave him. I remember when family, friends and colleagues compiled a book of letters to him in honor of his 70th birthday. Jephta wrote a warm, flowing two-page expression of love that made him cry when he first read it. I spent a long time composing a letter, which was short, too intellectual, forced, not what I wanted to express or felt. I was ashamed of it then and am ashamed of it today.

But I did dedicate my PhD thesis to him. He didn't know that until he opened the bound thesis and read "To Father" following the title page. He looked surprised and touched. That time calling him "Father" didn't seem stilted. There are times when the precise words mean less than their intent. I wasn't ashamed of my simple dedication and believe that it meant as much to him as it did to me. It was something I gave him that said in my own way that I was proud to be his son, that I loved him, and that he was an important part of my life and thesis, whether or not he understood science.

Papa's most extraordinary gift to me came in 1961 via a note scribbled on both sides of an unsealed envelope on which he states that he had bought the precious Batta Stradivarius cello (named after its first owner, Alexandre Batta) for me. I inherited the instrument after he died on August 6, 1976. It was his most prized possession. He wrote on that envelope that he trusted me to preserve it for mankind when he was gone. Papa didn't live by formal rules or behave conventionally. Everything was personal, like the hand-written note on the envelope. Papa's gifts were seldom wrapped, store-bought presents; they were personal treasures that were a part of him. I believe that Papa made me, through that envelope, a link in the history of music.

Papa wanted me to preserve the Batta cello and document his role in its history. Preservation was critical since the cello was old, made in 1714, the golden period of Stradivarius, and arguably the finest cello that he made. Although remarkably well preserved, apparently in part because it had been played relatively little, it could easily be damaged. As I write, the cello is safely displayed on loan at the Metropolitan Museum in New York for now. I had the cello renamed the Batta-Piatigorsky cello in two major published exhibitions. The first exhibition was in 1987 in Cremona, Italy, Stradivarius' birthplace, celebrating the 250th anniversary of his death; the second exhibition was in 2013 in the Ashmolean Museum in Oxford, England, which exhibited twenty-four of Stradivarius' finest string instruments. The cello is now officially known as the Batta-Piatigorsky cello, a fitting tribute that would have made Papa happy. That was something that I did for him.

Mama

Mama dozed off and on in her favorite armchair in the den as I sat on the soft sofa next to her, my back aching. Seven months earlier Mama had celebrated her hundredth birthday in good spirits and alert.

"Now 100, I'll start counting backwards," she had said.

Mama had organized her own birthday party, with a guest list of at least 50 people, half of whom were family, hired caterers, specified the menu, arranged for a tent on the back lawn for the guests, ordered flower arrangements. It was her only self-indulgent expense I can remember.

She was at the tail end of a mild case of pneumonia, as if any amount of pneumonia could be mild for someone 100 years old. Her blood pressure was low, her heart weak, her ankles swollen. She resisted going to a hospital, and I couldn't force that upon her. She was better off at home with her long-time loyal caretaker, Ianka Petrova (we called her Iana). To make Mama more comfortable, the doctor had given her oxygen. He was not optimistic about her recovery.

I wracked my mind what to say when she opened her eyes and looked at me. Why do we always assume that it's necessary to speak, to bring attention on ourselves or to put pressure for an answer? Small talk – the weather for example was meaningless. A dying person doesn't care about sunshine or rain. I mentioned the upcoming presidential campaign – she was an ardent Obama supporter – but political news had passed her by. She liked to talk about her five grandsons (Auran and Anton, and Jephta's children, Jonathan, Evan and Eric) and ten great grandchildren (Klara and Tobias from Auran and his wife, Tonje; Sivan, Dalia and Reuben from Anton and his wife, Ava; Julia, Benjamin and Rebecca from Jonathan and his wife, Paula; and Eli and Oliver from Evan and his wife, Joan), but she had difficulty remembering which of her great grandchildren belonged to which grandchild, even though we had made a flow chart with pictures to help her keep it straight.

Mama's adored pug, Sparky, stayed by her side day and night – love without words. Her tennis rackets were stored in the closet, and the television bestowing Mama a premier seat to watch Wimbledon and other major tennis championships in the past was idle. Piles of unread books would remain unread. A draft of my unpublished novel, *Jellyfish Have Eyes,* lay on the floor next to her. I had printed it with a large font for easy reading, but after a few pages she gave up, lacking the energy to continue reading. I am not sure she liked it anyway. She could be a tough critic, even in her reduced state.

Art dominated the house. Elegant stone sculptures of birds and abstract shapes Mama had carved over the last fifty years stood like proud gravestones throughout the house. Paintings I'd seen since childhood, mostly by impressionist and expressionist artists, decorated the walls, and African and oceanic masks and figures that my father had bought

rested on table tops and filled corners in her home. Photographs of Jephta and me as children and adults blended with those of Mama and Papa, and Babushka and Grandpapa, our children and grandchildren, and diverse friends
and acquaintances, and even some strangers, stared at me, mocking time and generational gaps.

Sure, Mama forgot some past events and current details, but don't we all as we age? She remained alert and observant, although confined to a wheel chair for a year or so. She noticed if I wore a new pair of socks or a belt or wrist watch she had not seen before. She asked about my health, despite her infirmities with age, and whether Lona was continuing her printing, and about Auran's work as a psychologist or Anton's latest production as a playwright. She welcomed friends and admirers who came to visit her. Although in need of a hearing aid, she recognized voices on the telephone and engaged, albeit concisely, in relevant conversation. She was the center of the family – symbol of stability – ever since Papa died 36 years earlier, and maybe even before that: Mama, the matriarch.

Two months after Lona and I returned home, Jephta and her husband Dan, who lived in Baltimore, went to visit Mama. Jephta called me from Los Angeles.

"How's she doing?" I asked.

"Not well. She's not eating and barely drinking, not enough to sustain her."

The end was in sight. Lona and I went back to Los Angeles the next day to see her once more before she died. Jephta and Dan and Iana and Catalina, Mama's house cleaner for many years, sat at her bedside when we arrived from the airport at six o'clock in the evening. She looked pale and small – shriveled – her eyes closed as she lay on her right side in the hospital bed that the hospice had brought to her home. Sedated with a trace of morphine, she breathed slowly and heavily.

"She looks just like Babushka," Jephta said. In my mind, I pictured Babushka in her early nineties after a stroke when Lona and I went to Paris with Mama to introduce her to 1-year-old Auran, her great grandson. Although I understood what Jephta saw in the physical resemblance between Mama and her mother Babushka, I was more impressed with how Mama was reduced to her shadow – a ghost of herself at best – not anyone I knew.

I put my hand on Mama's, which felt like dry skin on bone. "Lona and I are here to see you," I said.

I wanted to express more – tell her that I loved her – but I didn't. Maybe there were too many people about. I don't know. Intimacy needs privacy. Somehow saying aloud, "I love you," seemed empty, like "love you" after casual conversations or temporary good-byes that roll off the tongue like water on oil. However, just being there, thinking and feeling, did not seem enough. Yet, I remained silent. Such passing moments cannot be rescued.

We retired to the dining room to have dinner, while Iana remained with my mother. A few minutes later Iana appeared, looking drawn.

"I think she has stopped breathing," she said.

We went to see for ourselves. Dan, a neurologist, felt Mama's wrist.

"No pulse," he said.

Was it a coincidence that Mama postponed death until we arrived? Iana had asked her to hold off dying for just a little while until Lona and I came, that we were on the way. It would be like my mother to control death, to stare it down until she was ready. She was that type of person. She lived on her own terms. If she had waited to die until we came, she might have felt my hand on hers and heard me say that we were there to see her, although she gave no hint that she had felt or heard anything. But, who am I to know what fills a dying mind, or the mind of anyone for that matter? If I think Mama felt my silent love for a last good-bye, maybe that's enough.

I found it difficult to accept that Mama was gone. She was too strong a personality to disappear. Many people told me after her death how she had helped them by listening and understanding, by encouragement and advice, by helping financially.

It was uncanny how she felt what was hidden in my heart as a child or an adult. She read the expression on my face and my body language and knew whether I was sad or anxious or unhappy, even if I tried to bury it for one reason or another. She sensed what I was feeling by the tone of my voice on the telephone. I could never fool her, which was sometimes exasperating. She always said precisely what she thought whether it was what I wanted to hear or not. Discretion for her was silence – never false phrases in the guise of tact.

In our youth Jephta and I were very close to Mama, and she was close to us. To some extent, our childhood gave her a second chance for a happy childhood, which at times created a clumsy, unnatural relationship. She stayed with us when my father traveled on concert tours and never left our side and called us "the three musketeers." She swam with us at the beach, which she was never allowed to do as a girl because of a skin irritation (how dumb is that!), played tennis with us, and went horseback riding when Papa spent times in the summer in Tanglewood music center.

She was game for adventure. For example, when we were young teenagers, she arranged an overnight expedition with a guide in Switzerland hiking down the Jungfraujoch glacier and spending the night in a hut high in the mountain tops, despite that none of us had any experience for such an undertaking. It was an exhausting, enormous challenge. Crazy; yes, but an adventure I'll never forget. We were tied together by a rope to save us if we fell into a crevasse covered lightly by snow. We sank knee deep with every step in the soft afternoon snow, heard rumbles of avalanches in the distance, were cooked by the strong sun, and had to cling to the side of a cliff when dead-tired to reach the chalet. We rose at 4 in the morning to descend when the snow was solidly packed from the freezing night.

She helped me in many ways that I only touch on here with a few examples that seem trivial. Yet they are not. I remember wanting desperately to know how to swim when I was about four years old in Elizabethtown. She cracked a chicken wishbone with me after dinner one night and I wished that I knew how to swim. When I got the big piece – the winning piece – she said with such certainty that my wish would come true, I had no doubt that it would. I barely slept that night, excited to jump into the pristine Bouquet River in the morning. At the crack of dawn, off we went to see the miracle: I could swim! My mother's confidence in me and my confidence in her made it so.

And then there was the time that I played my first tennis tournament when I was fourteen and lost 6-0, 6-0, a humiliating experience. Nevertheless, she dwelled on the points I had won. "You'll do better next time," she said. "I'm sure." She had no doubt and she was right again, and I became a competitive junior tennis player in Southern California. Tennis became a bond between us. We won the Hotel del Coronado Mother/Son Tournament in San Diego once when I was a teenager.

Mama boosted my self-confidence throughout my life, which gave me a foundation of optimism beneath my pessimistic moments – and there was no shortage of those. Perhaps Mama's confidence in me compensated to some extent for her own insecurity, an outgrowth of her difficult childhood, when her parents entrusted her to a mean nanny rather than tell that they were proud of her, that she was able to achieve whatever she wanted. This, I surmise, may have made her take pleasure in my successes as her successes, adding pressure for me to succeed. I remember once hearing a radio interview of a young teenage girl who had just broken some swimming record.

"Was your mother thrilled to watch you set a new record?" asked the interviewer.

"Oh, no," she replied cheerfully. "I have eight siblings to feed, so my mom has no time to sit around watching me swim!"

I felt envious, both for her success and freedom. My mother came to all my tennis matches. Yet, Mama's devotion and belief in me, although constricting, provided focus and a trustworthy compass to steady my course.

Mama was my teacher up until the last years of her life. Her philosophy was simple: if you are not growing, you are dying. There is no status quo. I watched her experiment with new abstract styles of sculpting and new thoughts in her writing as she aged. Her article *Growing As We Age*, published in 2003, starts as follows: "Eighty-eight is said to be a good age. But the bones were not told, so on the tennis court they crackle like castanets. But in the studio, they are too busy to sing. Yes, eighty-eight still has future."

She always lived as if she had a future with more to do. I hadn't realized how powerful that idea was until I aged and found myself still driven to meet new challenges, such as writing after fifty years of science. Even at 96, she asked me for reassurance that she would not die young, as her brother Guy did at 98.

Taken aback, I said, "How can you die young? It's too late."

She smiled.

That is how I will remember her: smiling with a future.

Acknowledgements

I am indebted first and foremost to my remarkable parents for their love, positive influence, and belief in me.

Many scientists – mentors, postdoctoral fellows and colleagues – played key roles in the directions and ideas of my research throughout my career, and each has contributed invaluably to my scientific life recounted in this memoir. In particular, Harold Barnes, Leigh Hoadley, Albert Tyler, Alfred J. Coulombre, Charles Lowe, Philip Leder, and Joseph Horwitz are singled out. I am grateful to Jin Kinoshita, Carl Kupfer, Sheldon Miller, and Paul Sieving of the National Eye Institute for supporting my laboratory and giving me academic freedom to pursue research projects ranging from jellyfish to humans. Such freedom, which I do not take for granted, is at the heart of basic science and was responsible for productive twists and turns of my research.

The Writer's Center catalyzed my switch from science to writing. I thank Robert Bausch, Barbara Esstman, Kate Blackwell, Catherine Mayo, Elizabeth Poliner and William O'Sullivan for their excellent writing workshops. I am grateful to my fellow board members of The Writer's Center, especially James Mathews and Sally Mott Freeman, who provided a network that helped me assimilate into a writing life. I acknowledge with gratitude Robert Blumenthal, Michael Bustin, Richard Drachman, Bernadette Driscoll Engelstadt, Neal Gillen, Michael Hall, Sel Kardan, James Mathews, Warren Poland, Knud Ross, Stanton Samenow, Alan Schechter, and Hamid Shams, for reading parts or all of the manuscript, feedback, helpful advice, or stimulating conversations. In particular, I am grateful to Mía R. Garcia-Cortez for extensive discussions on the memoir, editing, arranging writing conferences and workshops for me to attend, guiding me in social media, contacting agents and querying publishers, and to Margaret Dimond for providing essential computer skills, often rescuing me from electronic meltdowns, advising me on matters of publication, and many constructive discussions. I am grateful to Adele Siegel for help in line editing.

I am greatly indebted to Barbara Esstman and Lucy Chumbley for crucial, expert editing. Both have independently edited the manuscript, made many useful suggestions for improvement, and helped mold drafts into a memoir.

I especially thank Van Andruss for encouraging me to write and publish a series of essays that formed the foundation of the book in his literary journal, *Lived Experience*.

I thank Stevan V. Nikolic for responding quickly and positively to my query for publication in Adelaide Books.

Finally, my wife Lona continually supported me while writing this memoir. She withstood my moody periods, read numerous drafts of the manuscript, and always gave helpful suggestions.

Joram Piatigorsky

About the Author

During his 50-year career at the National Institutes of Health, **Joram Piatigorsky** has published some 300 scientific articles and a book, *Gene Sharing and Evolution* (Harvard University Press, 2007), lectured worldwide, received numerous research awards, including the prestigious Helen Keller Prize for vision research, served on scientific editorial boards, advisory boards and funding panels, and trained a generation of scientists. Presently an emeritus scientist, he collects Inuit art, is on the Board of Directors of The Writer's Center in Bethesda, blogs (JoramP.com), and has published a series of personal essays in the journal Lived Experience and a novel, *Jellyfish Have Eyes* (IPBooks, 2014). He has two sons, five grandchildren, and lives with his wife in Bethesda, Maryland. He can be contacted at joram@joramp.com.

References

1. Elon, A.: Founder: *A Portrait of the First Rothschild and His Time* (Viking, 1996).

2. Muhlstein, A.: Baron James: *The Rise of the French Rothschilds* (The Vendome Press, New York, 1883).

3. Lottman, H. R.: *The French Rothschilds: The Great Banking Dynasty Through Two Turbulent Centuries* (Crown, 1995).

4. Piatigorsky, G.: *Cellist* (Doubleday, 1965).

5. de Rothschild, G.: Luigi Boccherini: *His Life and Work* (Oxford University Press, 1965).

6. Rothschild, M.: Dear Lord Rothschild: *Birds, Butterflies and History* (Balaban Publishers, Philadelphia, 1983).

7. Thomas, J.: *Birds, bugs and botany: a brief introduction to the world of the Rothschilds and Science* (The Rothschild Archive, Review of the Year April 2011 to March 2012, London).

8. Cahill, L.: *The World Writes to Walter: Cataloguing Tring's Correspondence* (The Rothschild Archives, Review of the Year April 2011 to March 2012, London).

9. Piatigorsky, J.: *Jump in the Waves* (St. Martin's Press, 1988).

10. Barnes, H., Finlayson, D. M. and Piatigorsky, J.: The effect of desiccation and anaerobic conditions on the behavior, survival general metabolism of three common cirripedes. Journal of Animal Ecology Vol. 32, 1963.

11. de Rothschild, G.: *The Whims of Fortune: The Memoirs of Guy de Rothschild* (Random House, 1985).

12. Watson, J.: *Avoid Boring People: Lessons from a Life in Science* (Vintage, 2010).

13. *Analysis of Development* (Editors, Benjamin Willier, Paul Weiss and Viktor Hamburger) (Saunders, Philadelphia, 1955).

14. Piatigorsky, J. and Whiteley, A. H.: A change in permeability and uptake of [14C]uridine in response to fertilization in Strongylocentrotus purpuratus eggs. Biochimica Biophysica Acta Vol. 108, 1965.

15. Piatigorsky, J. and Tyler, A.: Displacement of valine from intact sea urchin eggs by oxogenous amino acids. Journal of Cell Science Vol. 3, 1968.

16. Piatigorsky, J.: Studies on Nucleoside and Amino Acid Uptake and on RNA and Protein Synthesis by Growing Oocytes, Unfertilized and Fertilized Sea Urchin Eggs. Ph.D. Thesis, California Institute of Technology, 1967.

17. Developmental Biology, Vol. 21, 1970.

18. Piatigorsky, J. and Tyler, A.: Changes upon fertilization in the distribution of RNA containing particles in sea urchin eggs. Developmental Biology Vol. 21, 1970

19. Piatigorsky, J. Gametogenesis. In: *The Sea Urchin Embryo, Biochemistry and Morphogenesis* (Editor, G. Czihak) (Springer VerLag, 1975).

20. Solzhenitsyn, A.: *The First Circle* (Harpercollins, 1968).

21. Piatigorsky, J. and Rothschild, S. S.: Effect of serum on the synthesis of RNA and of DNA in the cultured lens epithelium of the chick embryo: Initiation of lens fiber formation in vitro. Biochimica Biophysica Acta Vol. 238, 1971.

22. Piatigorsky, J.: Insulin initiation of lens fiber differentiation in culture: Elongation of embryonic lens epithelial cells. Developmental Biology Vol. 30, 1973.

23. Bhat, S. P. and Piatigorsky, J.: Molecular cloning and partial characterization of δ- crystallin cDNA sequences in a bacterial plasmid. Proceedings of the National Academy of Sciences USA Vol. 76, 1979.

24. Jones, R. E., Bhat, S. P., Sullivan, M.A. and Piatigorsky, J.: Comparison of two δ-crystallin genes in the chicken. Proceedings of the National Academy of Sciences USA Vol. 77, 1980.

25. Chepelinsky, A.B., King, C.R., Zelenka, P.S. and Piatigorsky, J.: Lens specific expression of the chloramphenicol acetyltransferase gene promoted by 5' flanking sequences of the murine *a*A crystallin gene in explanted chicken lens epithelia. Proceedings of the National Academy of Sciences USA Vol. 82, 1985.

26. Overbeek, P.A., Chepelinsky, A.B., Khillan, J.S., Piatigorsky, J. and Westphal, H.: Lens-specific expression and developmental regulation of the bacterial chloramphenicol acetyltransferase gene driven by the murine *a*A crystallin promoter in transgenic mice. Proceedings of the National Academy of Sciences Vol. 82, l985.

27. Cajal, S. R.: *Advice for a Young Investigator* (A Bradford Book, MIT Press, 1999).

28. Keller, H.: *The Story of My Life* (Penguin, 1996).

29. Ingolia, T. D. and Craig, E. A.: Four small Drosophila heat shock proteins are related to each other and to mammalian alpha-crystallin. Proceedings of the National Academy of Sciences USA Vol. 79, 1982.

30. Horwitz, J.: Alpha-crystallin can function as a molecular chaperone. Proceedings of the National Academy of Sciences USA Vol. 89, 1992.

31. Piatigorsky, J. and Wistow, G.J.: Enzyme/crystallins: Gene sharing as an evolutionary strategy. Cell Vol. 57, l989.

32. Piatigorsky, J.: Lens crystallins. Innovation associated with changes in gene regulation. Journal of Biological Chemistry Vol. 267, 1992.

33. Piatigorsky, J., O'Brien, W.E., Norman, B.L., Kalumuck K., Wistow, G.J., Borras, T., Nickerson, J.M. and Wawrousek, E.F.: Gene sharing by δ-crystallin and argininosuccinate lyase. Proceedings of the National Academy of Sciences USA Vol. 85, l988.

34. Tomarev, S.I. and Piatigorsky, J.: Lens crystallins of invertebrates: diversity and recruitment from detoxification enzymes and novel proteins. European Journal of Biochemistry Vol. 235, 1996.

35. Tomarev, S.I., Callaerts, P., Koss, L., Zinovieva, R., Halder, G., Gehring, W. and Piatigorsky, J.: Squid Pax-6 and eye development. Proceedings of the National Academy of Sciences USA Vol. 94, 1997.

36. Piatigorsky, J., Horwitz, J., Kuwabara, T. and Cutress C.E.: The cellular eye lens and crystallins of Cubomedusan jellyfish. Journal of Comparative Physiology A Vol. l64, 1989.

37. Piatigorsky, J., Horwitz, J. and Norman, B.L.: J1-Crystallins of the cubomedusan jellyfish lens comprise a novel family encoded in at least three intronless genes. Journal of Biological Chemistry Vol. 268, 1993.

38. Kozmik, Z, Ruzickova, J., Jonasova, K., Matsumoto, Y., Vopalensky, P., Kozmikova, I., Strnad, H., Kawamura, S., Piatigorsky, J., Paces, V. and Vlcek, C.: Assembly of the Cnidarian camera-type eye from vertebrate-like components. Proceedings of the National Academy of Sciences USA, Vol. 105, 2008.

39. Piatigorsky, J.: *Gene Sharing and Evolution*: The Diversity of Protein Functions (Harvard University Press, 2007).

40. Lewis, M.: *The Undoing Project: A Friendship that Changed Our Minds* (W.W. Norton & Company, 2016).

41. Medawar, P. B.: *Advice to a Young Scientist* (Harper Colophon Books, Harper & Row, 1979).

42. Piatigorsky, J.: *The Spirit Makes All the Difference*. NIH Catalyst, May-June, 2000.

43. Piatigorsky, J.: Gene sharing in lens and cornea: facts and implications. Progress in Retinal and Eye Research Vol. 17, 1998.

44. *Molecular Biology of the Eye: Genes, Vision, and Ocular Disease* (Editors, Joram Piatigorsky, Toshimichi Shinohara and Peggy S. Zelenka) (Alan R. Liss, 1988).

45. Piatigorsky, J.: Gene expression and genetic engineering in the lens. Friedenwald lecture. Investigative Opthalmology and Visual Science 28, 1987.

46. Cohen, H., *You Can Negotiate Anyth*ing (Bantam; Reissue edition, 1982)

47. Piatigorsky, J.: *Jellyfish Have Eyes* (International Psychoanalytic Books, 2014).

48. Shurkin, J.: Science and Culture: Using fiction to make the case for basic research. Proceedings of the National Academy of Sciences USA, Vol. 112, 2015.

CPSIA information can be obtained
at www.ICGtesting.com
Printed in the USA
BVHW031348110321
602277BV00017B/789/J

9 781949 180534